BIBLICAL *Women* AS ENABLERS

DR. STEPHEN HARRISON
AND RICHARD HUIZINGA

Copyright © 2025 by Dr. Stephen Harrison and Richard Huizinga.

ISBN: 979-8-89465-125-5 (sc)
ISBN: 979-8-89465-126-2 (e)

All rights reserved. No part of this publication may be reproduced, distributed, or transmitted in any form or by any means, including photocopying, recording, or other electronic or mechanical methods, without the prior written permission of the author, except in the case of brief quotations embodied in critical reviews and certain other noncommercial uses permitted by copyright law.

Printed in the United States of America.

Integrity Publishing
39343 Harbor Hills Blvd Lady Lake, FL 32159

www.integrity-publishing.com

CONTENTS

Preface vii

Women As Enablers viii

Introduction xi

Analogy And Metaphors 1
   God As Metaphor 1
   The Analogy Of Fascia And Creation 3
   Creation, Feminine Metaphors, and More 5
   Using Bitter For Better Or Badder 6
   Women And Gnosticism 8
   Jesus And Sophia 10
   Throwing Stones Or Walking Away 12
   Yeast And The Bread Of Life 14
   Woman Why Do You Cry? 16

Genesis Part 1 19
   Women And God. Encounters And Questions 19
   When God Endorsed Blame And Cursed 21
   When The Sons of God Had Fun And God Was Sorry 23
   The Short Shrift Of Women Of Genesis – Part 1 24
   The Short Shrift Of Women Of Genesis – Part 2 26
   The Creation Of Blame – Part 1 28
   The Angel Of The Lord 29
   The Creation Of Blame – Part 2 31
   The Sister 33

Genesis Part 2 35
    Same Father 35
    Laughter 36
    Sarah's Legacy 37
    A Wife for Isaac 38
    Jacobs's wives 39
    Rebekah's Wishes 41
    Did Rebekah love Esau? 42
    Joseph, Women, And The Economy Of
    The Original Testament. 43
    Joseph, Women Economy Part 2 45

Other Original Testament 48
    Holy Moses: Women Who Disobeyed 48
    Miriam, Sister Of Moses 49
    Esther. 53
    Kings And Beautiful Women 57
    Women And Risk Taking 60
    Righteousness And Women 62
    Deborah, Judge And Prophetess And More 64
    Hosea And Gomer 66
    A Surprisingly Powerful Woman 68

Job 71
    Job And Women 71
    Anachronistic Moralism 73
    Anachronistic Sexism 73
    Job's Code 74
    Adultery 1 75
    Adultery 2 76
    Adultery 3 77
    Job's Conclusion 1 78
    Job's Conclusion 2 78
    Job's Conclusion 3 79
    Job's Conclusion 4 80

David And Solomon 81
The Most Powerful Women In David's Life 81
David's Motivation 82
David's Anger Over Family Incest And Rape 84
Women of David 85
The Woman From Tekoa 87
David And The Make Believe Woman 90
David And The Pivotal Woman 92
Solomon: Wisdom, Prostitutes, And Unwed Mothers – Part 1 ... 94
Solomon: Wisdom, Prostitutes, And Unwed Mothers – Part 2 ... 95

New Testament Part 1 98
Born Of A Woman – Part 1 98
Born Of A Woman – Part 2 100
Born Of A Woman – Part 3 (The Meaning Of Christmas) ... 101
Easter And The Women 103
The Transformative Power Of Jesus 108
The Woman Who Saved Paul's Life 110
Mary And Martha Revisited 112
The Upper Room 113
Healing Women 115

New Testament Part 2 117
True Healing 117
Women In High And Low Places 119
Women Uplifted 120
Parable Gender Part 1 121
Parable Gender Part 2 123
Parable Gender Part 3 125
Women and Union with God as seen in Parables 128
Mark From Advent To Resurrection 130
Resurrection Summary 131

Women With Questionable Backgrounds 134
All In The Family 134
Hagar, Seen By God 135
God Is Speaking 137

Women Of Ill Repute. 139
Jesus Solicits A Woman Of Ill Repute 141
The Birth Of Forgiveness New Testament 143
Washing Jesus Feet 145
Woman Caught In Adultery 146
Hagar And Forgiveness 147

Conclusion. **149**

PREFACE

When Rich and I chose our title as Biblical Women as Enablers, we were met with some reluctance of this choice. Many people have come to understand the word enable as a negative connotation, particularly of people who have addictive types of behavior. This meaning is certainly not our intention, as we very much mean this to be a positive book of the accomplishments of women who have enabled other women and men to reach for a higher goal and to attain it. This distinction of two meanings that are opposite in nature is separate from our use of offensive in our work Parables and Paradox: The Offensive Gospel wherein we definitely wished to imply the duo meanings of offensive.

In fact, the Oxford English dictionary gives the word enable as meaning the authority or means to do something. A second definition is to make something operational or to activate it. The word enabler is listed as a derivative in the noun form which does not change its effective meaning. Even the definition that the Oxford English dictionary gives of an enabling act is not one of a negative connotation. Rather, it is a statute empowering a person or body to take certain action, especially to make regulations rules or orders. It is not clear how the term enabler came to become negative over time, but it is not our purpose here to go through that historical evolution. Rather our purpose here is to focus on a positive way that women have enabled various people to accomplish positive measures that have been overlooked. We hope this clarification enables you to enjoy stories of women that are under recognized or under appreciated

Women As Enablers

Sometimes Rich and I do not determine the title of a book until it has been written. To be clear, there are certain themes that we have in mind that we hope that the title will reflect well at the same time perhaps enticing some people because of the catchy nature of the title. Waiting for the title development while writing has the advantage of not being locked in to a particular theme, but rather letting the material develop where it flows naturally.

An early working title for this book was Women and the Short Shrift. A more catchy title was Eve-olution. Of course, what we would like with such a title is to show how far women have come since Eve in the garden and absorbing blame. The sad reality is that when this book was completed, we could not really say that the Bible represents a chronological development leading to the advancement of women. To be clear, there appear to be epiphanies and breakthroughs for women. Sometimes these seem to be God inspired, and other times led by women. It is a rare occasion, though that the advances are promoted by men.

By the same token, we raise the question of where would we be as a people without the women and types of women that we have represented in this book. We do not normally think of the word enabling being positive because it is used in the negative context so often in our daily language. To enable someone often means to allow someone to continue to perform less than wholesome acts and duties which they perhaps would not do if they did not have their enablers. Of course there is a positive context for which we wish to appeal.

If we turn to the story of David, we might come up with several classic enablers and several subtle enablers who are women. Micah enables David to escape with his life, only to be later turned on in a rather vengeful fashion after he marries her. This happens on several occasions for which we encourage the reader to take a look at our work, entitled David and Michelangelo. Bathsheba enables the power-hungry womanizer David to kill her own husband. She will in turn be consoled by David when she uses loses their mutual baby by having sex with him.

Moses is enabled by his sister and numerous other women to become the effective leader he ultimately does. Hagar enables Abraham to experience the joy of a child and keep his hopes alive for the child and nation that God has promised Abraham. Ruth enables her daughter-in-law to do some questionable measures to snare a husband. Eve enables Adam to believe that he can experience wisdom and become like God. As we can see several of these examples have the negative connotation of enabling while occasionally pointing to the positive aspect.

Well and good. That was all Original Testament story. What about the New Testament? How does the woman at the well enabled well enable Jesus? How does the woman caught in the act of adultery enable Jesus? The first part of the answer might simply be that they were in the right place at the right time. The second part of the answer might be that they allowed Jesus the occasion to correct an injustice by being themselves. The third part is more subtle in that they accept the forgiveness that Jesus offers on the spot and allow themselves to be transformed. We may not have the luxury of the first two conditions, but if we allow ourselves to be transformed like the foreign woman who worked hard to get close to Jesus, then we can overcome the obstacles that allow for transformation.

INTRODUCTION

Normally, when we look at a preface or introduction, we are interested in the authors perspective on the main topic. Perhaps there will be some wandering in the wilderness like Moses as they bring us to the thesis. They ultimately arrive at their perspective, but it will, like an ancient treasure, buried somewhere in there. For those looking for such treasure here I am not certain that it will be found. You see I feel that this is a book that we need to write and have a fair number of ideas but don't really know what the overarching theme is other than it is about women. This book will draw on earlier material that we have written on, often with my colleague, Rich Huizinga.

We will certainly talk about the feminine spirit right alongside the female perspective. This work will not be about the systematic cover-up of the role of women and the feminine in biblical history, but we do suggest that this becomes evident with little more than a cursory review. One need look no further than the creation story to see both the expression, and then later the suppression of the feminine spirit. We have indeed included our earlier essay that we feel captures this. If we may state a thesis it is this in that our goal is to look at both familiar and unfamiliar stories of women, through the eyes of inclusiveness, and accordingly to gain insights into how this may help us today with our approach to social justice.

We will look during this work at the usual, strong female characters of the Bible. We will come to see some of them in a different light not merely employing the microscopic perspective, but the more global perspective. To do so it may be helpful to turn on our eastern perspective and look at the interconnectedness rather than the solitary, as is so often the case in western culture. By the same token, we will review the potential significance of many women who are unheralded other than a passing note. We will see that Jesus may have learned a key element about forgiveness from his earthly symbolic father Joseph, when he perhaps, forgave a woman in a way that you have not perceived previously.

Perhaps we can intrigue you here when we asked you to consider, who was the first woman who was described as being loved by her partner. Furthermore, we might ask who is the only woman in the Bible, who is said, specifically to love a man. What price did she pay for that love and why does she not get more credit in history other than basically a footnote. Who is the only woman in the Bible or for that matter of either sex to actually rename God? Who is the only woman in all of the Scriptures to be ascribed the ability to actually write and what is the significance of that? This, by the way, is not to take away from the significance of the wonderful work by Harold Bloom, entitled the book of J in which a woman has written extensively on now familiar stories.

The book of J makes a very key point for the power of the feminine perspective not only in the biblical sense, but all of western literature. It is after all the educated and detective surmise by Professor Bloom, that much of the key element of the Original Testament was written by a female, specifically in the court of king David. We will not defend his thesis here, except to say that it is a book very worthy of exploring to see the implications of that. Speaking of David, we will demonstrate it quite possibly he fought Goliath as much to obtain the favor of a woman, as he did, to redeem the undersized army of Israel against the Philistines. There is a reason, of course, for this feminine perspective to be presented in the way that it was. We have examined how various stories may be kept alive by the different sexes in our work on Parables.

As per our usual style, we have very few references as we like the average reader to be able to come to the same conclusions or understanding, or appreciation that we do without having much to reference. That having been said the book Womanist Midrash by Wilda Gafney was inspirational and served a good source for several stories in the Original Testament. For the New Testament, the book, Short Stories by Jesus written by Amy- Jill Levine will be most helpful as a reference. In that book, we will see that Jesus is ultimately concerned about priorities and relationships and social justice. This includes men and women. Our work will not propose to use gender inclusive language, where it is not applicable, though we will indeed show some fundamental roots of the female influence that has been buried.

ANALOGY AND METAPHORS

God As Metaphor

We are told in the first book of the Bible, namely Genesis that we are made in the image of God. Yet we really do not get the image of God in the book of Genesis. We are only told that humans were created male and female in the God image. In fact, the image and story of God appears to evolve over time as noted in the Pulitzer Prize book God, a history by Jack Miles. We find it both essential and somewhat effective to speak of God in terms of metaphors. Marcus Borg will describe several of those metaphors for God in his book: Meeting Jesus Again for the First Time.

Borg points out that there were no video cameras for the Easter story. Accordingly, he knows that it is important to view the Easter story as a metaphorical narrative, which is still very rich with meaning. Instead of looking at the Easter story as the resuscitation of a dead body, we rather see resurrection as a metaphor for transformation. Indeed, the story of Jesus, appearing on the road to Emmaus is not so much about a particular event, but rather as a story narrative of how Jesus travels besides us with a presence that we often do not recognize or realize.

Jesus employs the metaphor of bondage for the human condition. This bondage process would have been something that the Jewish tradition of his day recognized as part of the triad of tradition. This involved the liberation of Moses in the book of Exodus and the liberation from the Babylon exile, and finally the priestly role. Indeed, Easter represents the defeat of these inferior to God powers. The apostle

Paul extends the metaphor of crucifixion by noting metaphorically that he has been crucified with Christ, just as Jesus himself noted that to be his follower of truth that one must deny themselves and take up their cross and follow the truth of Jesus.

Jesus as sacrifice is a metaphor that God has already taken care of whatever it is we think separates us from God. We are made right with God by noting that Jesus is the metaphorical sacrifice which abolishes the system of requirements originally presented in the Original Testament. Jesus instructs us to be compassionate as God is compassionate. This word compassion comes from an image like a womb in the Jewish tradition. Therefore, in order to understand the image that Jesus portrayed of God; we must necessarily understand the feminine metaphors.

We must keep in mind that the original metaphors for God that the original church employed following the Easter event was the father/son imagery as well as the wisdom/Sophia/feminine energy and imagery. Even the use of justification by Christians is a metaphor. When we look at the sacrifice of Jesus as a metaphor that replaces the absurd notion of propitiating an angry God by blood, then we have come to the powerful truth of the Christian message. Indeed, the book of Hebrews uses the metaphor of Jesus as the high priest who makes the sacrifice in order that we do not have to make the type of traditional sacrifices originally required.

Ultimately, death and resurrection, as represented by Jesus, serve as revelation of the way of transformation to new life. Accordingly, death and resurrection are the ultimate metaphors of the Christian experience. The internal death leads to a new identity as expressed by Paul who said that it is no longer I who live, but Christ who lives in me. This is also the meaning of Jesus when he says that if anyone wants to follow him that they must deny themselves and take up their cross and follow him. The sacrifice of Jesus makes God immediately accessible. It is only when we sacrifice our own limited understanding of God and recognize the wisdom of God known as Sophia, that we may have the peace that comes from the acknowledgment of metaphorical truth.

The Analogy Of Fascia And Creation

The connective tissue fascia is one of those mysteries of medicine in the human being that you don't hear much about. This is in itself rather amazing in the sense that fascia connects literally everything from our head to toe in a connective tissue type of pattern. Paradoxically it both connects and separates various compartments of the human body. It tends to get a bad rap in conditions like plantar fasciitis. Adhesions also are part of its problematic presentation. Likely we don't hear more about the fascia because we don't have a medicine or pill for it or a surgery directly impacting its outcome for our benefit.

Our purpose here is to use the fascia as a type of analogy for the story of creation. All of creation is interconnected. It all begin out of chaos from what we might think of as a dense web of interconnective tissue much like fascia is. Yet when God performed the creation, it was with the notion that things had to be separated, even while they were connected. So, God first creates heaven and earth. These seem rather distinct, but they remain interconnected. So too do we have the creation of dark and light. So too, do they seem opposite and yet they remain interconnected. Then we have land and water to seemingly different substances, and yet they too are interconnected, even as they are separated. So, on the list we go

Out of this amorphous mass comes life. Arguably plant life first much as evolutionary science describes, and then next animal life beginning with rudimentary forms. Finally, we have the creation of human beings. It is both convenient and prejudiced to recall only one creation story in which the male is created first when in reality Genesis has 2 creation accounts. However, the more primordial version is that which is presented first in Genesis chapter 1. There God creates male and female in the image of God. Of course, God cannot create something in God's own image unless God has the elements of male and female present within. Arguably the creation story told in Genesis chapter 2 must be interpreted as has been pointed out by many as that the original Adam is actually both male and female initially. Then a separation begins, which has the apparent distinctions that we recognize today.

In the second version of the creation, story found in Genesis chapter 2 we see that the formula for the creation of the first prototype human being is that of creation from the dust along with breath. Then, just as God must have sensed that it was not good to be alone, so too did God realize that the first prototype human being would be best suited to have complimentary parts in the form of another actual being. . This "another" is then interpreted as the first female. Really, though it is clear even in the second version that the female prototype is split or separated from the first prototype human being. At this point of creation, the male and female appear to take walks together and gather fruit together and later sew things together. They do not view themselves as distinct from one another, and really do not even know that they are naked.

Then there is a challenge from one of God's creatures. This is most commonly mythologically represented as a serpent. The appeal of the serpent is that human beings=do not accept the image for which they have been made into. They wish to be Other than what they were created to be. It is not merely wishing to have more or wishing to have knowledge, but rather to be Other , other than which they were created. The fact that they wish to be more like God in whose image they were made is not really the point here. Rather it is that they wish to be Other then they were created.

So now we have another view of the so-called original sin, as wishing to be other than in the image for which we were created. Now the human beings see themselves as different from each other, and naked, and the need to cover up something. It is human beings, who begin the process of blame once that they have discovered that there is something different and other than themselves. They blame the serpent who represents darkness, even though God very much created the darkness, and kept it somewhat connected, even as it separated it much as our fascia did above. The mythology of the curse comes in that the female will crush the head of the serpent just as the female today needs to crush anything which tries to make itself different or other or better than it's original image was. Meanwhile, the serpent by striking the heel of the woman, appears to have inflicted the first case of plantar fasciitis.

Creation, Feminine Metaphors, and More

For this essay, we will examine some unique angles for the role of women in the creation story in general as well as the creation of the church. We will rely on the work by Amy and Jill Levine entitled The Bible with and without Jesus, as well as the work by Richard Rohr: Jesus Alternative Play. We begin with our creation perspective that includes a feminine spirit and the word "us" as we have written on elsewhere. Amy Jill Levine points out that the Jewish perspective has long included the reference to "us" as the God figure speaking to lady wisdom, which is often personified by the name Sophia.

Additional support for the feminine in the nature of God is cited by Amy Jill Devine in the Hebrew noun often used for the spirit. This is the word Ruach which has only a feminine form, unlike other languages, which translate both masculine and feminine. Of course, the implications for the feminist perspective are endless with this. She goes on to mention that in the book of Genesis in the creation story, the word used for God, Elohim, is grammatically plural. Only later in the Jewish community does the term derive to the limits of the masculine only.

Richard Rohr helps add some perspective to the creation story. He notes that at the end of each day of creation that God typically calls everything as good. However, this terminology of good is not applied to the second day of creation in which heaven is separated from earth. This he notes is symbolic of the tearing apart of the union of not only heaven and earth, but also that which is sacred from that which is secular. It becomes the duty of religion to reconnect darkness and light and to reconnect earth, and heaven, along with so many other seemingly opposite elements.

These complementary elements would include the masculine and feminine reconnection as was noted in the original one body from which they were created. Towards his conclusion Richard Rohr notes that human history is all about the disconnection between the personal stories and the great universal story of connectedness. The little stories of disconnect include the disconnection between nations along with ethnicity. The disconnection includes the great disconnect that has been perpetrated and perpetuated by religion between the sexes, as well as to orientation.

Rohr who is Catholic, suggests that if we had a more feminine image of God that we might have understood creation as more of a childbirth and labor of birth experience. Indeed, this image is presented by no less than the apostle Paul in Romans 8:22. There we read that the whole creation has been groaning as in the pains of childbirth. He uses this metaphor to compare with the adoption by the assistance of the Spirit. It is the Jewish writer, Amy Jill-Levine, who points out that the rock associated with Peter and the creation of the Catholic Church, uses the masculine for his name but the feminine for the rock on which the church was to be built.

She also quotes Elizabeth Katie Stanton, who was born over 200 years ago. There she mentions the reference that the story of creation is a gradually ascending story beginning with creeping things and then great sea monsters followed by birds and then cattle and other living things. Then we have the creation of man followed by the combination of creation in the creation of woman. This she notes as in much of the theme of the Bible is echoed by Jesus in which what is done last and not first can be more important much as was shown with his first miracle at the wedding.

Using Bitter For Better Or Badder

Our essay for today has to do with comparing the bitterness of Job with the bitterness of Naomi. There is no question that they are both bitter as along the way they both attach adjectives like bitterness to their struggles or at least the correlative of those adjectives. In fact, Naomi will rename herself Mara, which means bitterness. This is opposed to her original name of Naomi, which meant Pleasant. Both will attach their outcomes of bitterness to actions that God has taken against them. We really have nothing to counter that in the scriptures. Indeed, the concluding chapter of Job states that God brought these troubles upon Job.

Our argument in this essay is not about whether they deserved their struggles or what they did to deserve such action. Indeed, Job is listed as upright and, in some texts, listed as perfect. Meanwhile,

Naomi seems to have had a very limited action role only to be the recipient of such drastic misfortune. The majority of her story comes in the first of the four short chapters in the book of Ruth. There we are told that she has first lost her husband and then a short while later she has lost her two sons, who married foreign women in the area where Naomi had sojourned during a famine with her husband. Upon the loss of both her partner, and apparently the only two children, how could she not be anything but bitter.

This might not strike us as first at first, because when she is getting ready to return to her homeland, Naomi tells the two daughter-in-law's who wish to come with her that they need to stay. She even offers them a blessing for the Lord to show kindness to them, just as they have shown kindness to her. There is no mention of kindness being shown by the Lord to Naomi. Indeed, in just a few short verses, we are told that it was more bitter for her than for the daughter-in-law's because the hand of the Lord had gone out against her. Even then she had not adopted yet, the name of Mara, which means bitterness, though she certainly could have made her case at that point.

Most of us might think at that point that if the person that we are trying to follow is blaming the God that she believes in and who herself is urging you not to follow her, that perhaps we had best take that course of action. However, Ruth pleads with Naomi, her mother-in-law, to let her follow and to have her people be her and Naomi's God to be the god of Ruth. In fact, she suggests that God may deal severely with herself if anything but death separates her from Naomi. It is only when she returns to her hometown of Bethlehem, City of David, and ultimately Jesus that she changes her name to Mara.

Now let us in contrast to the story in Job. Again, our purpose here is not to question Job and his uprightness. nor is it to question God, who either allows affliction to be extreme to show as we were suggested in the earlier chapters, or is the direct promoter behind it, as we are told in the concluding chapter number 42. Rather we wish to see both what Job is actually bitter about and also what he does with his bitterness.

Although, technically Job does not ever curse God, which is the prediction of Satan and the recommendation of his own wife, he arguably curses with strong language, many other things. He curses the day he was born, starting, in chapter 3, even though he will suffer no further afflictions after chapter 2. Job appears to be very bitter about the fact that his friends do not comfort him in the way that he desires and do not consider him to be blame free as he believes himself to be. Job is very bitter about the loss of his reputation. He is bitter to the point that he feels abandoned by his family and his own wife. Nowhere, do we find him mentioning bitterness about the loss of his faithful servants, or for that matter for the loss of all of his children.

Ask yourself, whose bitterness serves the better purpose here. Is it the bitterness of Naomi who may not have had much to begin with or is it the bitterness of Job who obviously was blessed as recognized by both Satan and God. After all, Job's three faithful friends, who are his strong support system, will sit silently in mourning for seven days while Job bitterly decries his losses. They are never impressed with the faith that Job has. In fact, even after Job is commanded to pray for them in the concluding chapter, we do not see evidence of removal of bitterness, perhaps on either side. By the same token, we have a woman who did not have much, and had lost all and had no obvious friends in a foreign land who had the influence despite her own personal bitterness, such that this widowed young woman Ruth, in need of a partner, would come home and adopt the God that a woman such as Naomi adhered to even in her uttermost loss.

WOMEN AND GNOSTICISM

Elaine Pagels has written a book, entitled the Gnostic Gospels, which was a winner of the national book award. We highly commend this book to you in order to understand some appreciation for the feminine element n the Bible including that was often present in the early church. as Elaine Pagel's notes in this work. It was once very difficult to distinguish certain elements of the gnostic approach to that of what later became orthodox Christianity. This recognition is important, because the mere mention of gnostic roots, often conjures up blasphemy and heresy among even scholars today.

The Gnostic book known as the triple-formed Primal Thought celebrates the traditional, feminine powers of thought and foresight. This feminine energy exists in every female and Is primordial to all being. Elaine Pagels points out that the gnostic text Thunder, Perfect

Mind provides a powerful poem, spoken from the feminine divinity. In that work, we see the contrast between the first and last and many other opposites incorporated in this feminine spirit. Meanwhile the gnostic gospel of Mary echoes the traditional gospels of Mark and John in that Mary Magdalene was the first to see the risen Christ.

Our purpose in employing her work is to illustrate the role of the feminine through the eyes of the gnostics. The gnostics have the audacity to point out that what most Christians naïvely worship as created in God, the Father is only one image of the true God. The gnostic tradition recognizes the true source of divine power, as being the depth of all being. This ultimately leads to discovery of one's spiritual origins, which include the true father and true mother. In this gnostic sect, both men and women participated in the opportunity to be selected as priest or bishop or prophets.

In recognizing the role of the feminine the gnostic influence did not borrow from the pagan traditions of the mother goddess, but rather used rather specific Christian and Jewish heritage, which they expanded to embrace, both masculine and feminine elements. Some of the gnostics prayed to both the father and the mother. Indeed, among the gnostics, there were three approaches to explain the divine. One was in the form of the masculofeminine, which was all one source. The second group claimed that any sexual language was only to be employed as a metaphor, since the divine is neither male nor female. A third group chose to use either masculine or feminine, depending on the context.

The gnostic tradition relied on the distinction of true from false, not by the relationship to the clergy of the church, or even the apostles themselves, but rather on the understanding of its members. Right alongside this characteristic is the relationship that fellow Gnostics had with each other. Enlightened Gnostics were able to discriminate true from false themselves without having to go through an intermediary. They emphasized the true union its members enjoyed with God, and with one another.

There may be many reasons that the gnostic Christianity did not survive. This extends beyond the fact that it was condemned as heresy by the church at large. Part of the problem that the gnostics had was that their pathway was largely available only to the intellectual or spiritual elite. Mainstream Christianity offered inclusion for many. In addition, orthodox Christianity provided food for the poor and buried their dead. However, when we threw out the bathwater of gnosticism, we threw out the baby as well. That baby contained seed from the mother as well as seed from the father.

JESUS AND SOPHIA

For this section, we are indebted to Marcus Borg for his book: Meeting Jesus Again For The First Time. Borg points out that historically that there were complementary images of Jesus in the early church. There was the Jesus as male as son of God. Simultaneously, there was Jesus, as representing the wisdom of God that was first portrayed in the Original Testament as the feminine Sophia. While perhaps the strongest representation of the feminine Sophia wisdom comes in the book of Proverbs, this theme is indeed prevalent in the Original Testament.

First, we begin with the premise that Jesus was a purveyor of wisdom. Wisdom expressed itself in the form of parables as well as aphorisms. The beauty of the parables is that they are wisdom that prevails over time. They are first and foremost story, and not to be taking literally. As Borg notes the stories were likely changed and modified and told in several different fashions, even during the early church before they became codified Into theology. In our own work on Parables and Paradox, we pointed out which parables were likely kept alive in the telling and retelling by women and those that were kept alive by men.

Borg notes that Jesus was not primarily a teacher of information or even of morals. He really did not bring any new belief system about God. Rather Jesus came to promote the Way of transformation. This transformation displaced conventional wisdom to that of a God centered wisdom. As such Jesus emphasized the portion of Judaism of alternative wisdom which emphasized grace over the law. This form of alternative consciousness is often overlooked in the expressions of Christian theology which often convey covert if not overt antisemitism.

In medicine, we refer to the embryo stage as the early development of the human body. Embryonic Christology included Jesus as the embodiment or incarnation of the wisdom of God, right alongside of the son to father relationship. The personification of wisdom culminates in the Original Testament book of Proverbs, with the name most commonly transmitted as Sophia. There we read that her role in creation was being with God in the beginning before the world was created.

Sophia is also noted to be a host of a banquet. This banquet imagery was employed by Jesus, both in real life to a significant degree whether his first miracle at a wedding changing water to wine performance or with tax collectors and other so-called sinners. The banquet imagery also works its way into several parables. In the book known as the Wisdom of Solomon, likely written near the time of Jesus, we see that Sophia is spoken of as a unique and intelligent and subtle entity who loves goodness and is irresistible and beneficent, steadfast, and all powerful and penetrating through all the spirits.

The role of Sophia is far more important than merely a literary device of personification. Indeed, as we see in the message above, the attributes of Sophia are indistinguishable from God in general. Indeed, it is not simply personification of wisdom in the female form, but more importantly, personification of God in the female form. The synoptic gospels carry this image of the feminine compassion of God through the message of Jesus. The personification of God, as Sophia suggests that God is like a woman, and that Jesus is a spokesperson for the combined compassion of Sophia and God.

The ultimate expression of imagery of God comes through the gospel of John. When we substitute the word logos for the word which became flesh, we see a close connection with the wisdom of God, as expressed through the feminine Sophia of the Original Testament. John is effectively saying that the logos or Sophia that is wisdom rather than Jesus was what was present before creation. Indeed, scholars have been long aware of the connection between the logos of John and Sophia in the traditional Jewish religion. Borg then extends this connection to open the book of John with this phrasing: in the beginning was Sophia, and the Sophia was with God and Sophia was God.

Even the apostle Paul recognized these types of connections when he talked about being made right with God by grace as opposed to justification by works. Paul also recognizes the connection with Jesus through whom all things were made indeed according to his traditional Jewish upbringing. Paul uses the language of Sophia. Therefore, according to both the gospel of John and Paul, that which was present in Jesus, in the beginning was the Sophia of God. Early Christianity preserved this dual incarnation of Jesus, coming from the father in the personal expression of Abba as personal daddy as well as being the prodigy of Sophia.

Both historical research and practical application reveal that God can only be discovered as metaphor, and never fully or exactly described. As difficult as it may be for some traditional Christians to fathom, Jesus is not literally the son of God, though Jesus may be spoken, metaphorically in such terminology, just as Jesus may be spoken of as the Sophia or wisdom of God. If we are to be at home with God both now and eternally, we must in the words of Robert Frost be at home with the metaphor. We will have more to say about this in our next essay.

Throwing Stones Or Walking Away

Although the first part of John chapter 8 does not appear in some of the oldest manuscripts, experts feel that this is one of the most reliable stories of authentic nature as far as the gospel goes . The simplicity of the story along with the resonance of Jesus message of forgiveness is demonstrated as well here as any story in the gospel. With that in mind, we might do well to have another look at the story and it's potential many layers like other gospel stories.

Seemingly the set up behind the story is that of the religious leaders of the day trying to entrap Jesus by getting him to go against a very basic and long-standing commandment from the original testament days that would have been very much embedded in Jesus own mind. Before we fall too far into condemning the religious leaders involved, we would have us invoke the thought process of Amy Jill- Levine . She has us to consider that whenever there is a confrontation of Jesus with the religious leaders of avoiding the antisemitism that is instilled and often emanates and permeates not only the story, but our way of thinking to this day.

We must keep in mind that Jesus had gone to the temple for a variety of reasons. No doubt one of them was to worship. Another outcome of this visit to the temple was that he sat down to talk to people who had come out in the numbers to see him and hear him. Jesus would have been coming to bring depth and clarity to the Jewish traditions rather than contradict them. These new interpretations of Jesus would be no more threatening and no less threatening than those challenges that arise in any structured organization or philosophy or science in any age.

Although we are told that the set up with the woman caught in the act of adultery was in order for the leaders to entrap Jesus, we must be cautious about accepting this interpretation of a story that had been told orally for quite some time before it was written down. We must allow for the distinct possibility that the religious leaders were looking for a better interpretation of someone caught in the act of adultery than what the law of Moses allowed for. Perhaps they wished to add some level in order to vindicate themselves for not having put anyone to death for the act of adultery as they had been commanded to.

Yes, you read that right. There are no recorded instances of anyone having been put to death for the act of adultery from the time Moses gave such a law until the time of Jesus. Likely they knew the woman as a well-known adulterous. Accordingly catching her was something that was readily done and perhaps even staged to a degree. They may well have brought the woman to Jesus in that setting for their own clarity. Even for their own justification and rationalization for not having stoned anyone to death that they knew to be involved in the act of adultery.

Jesus at first seems to ignore their basic question but instead writes something unknown in the dirt. There has been plenty of speculation as to what the unknown writing may have been, but that will not add to our perspective here. Rather Jesus merely challenges them to go ahead and throw the first stone, beginning with a person among them who is without sin. Here we must allow that the reference may well be that of a sexual sin. Here we must allow that while they may not have committed the physical act of adultery as is sometimes suggested in reference to the writing in the dust, but that they had heard Jesus statement that whoever looks at a woman lustfully has already committed adultery in his heart.

We are intrigued naturally by the reference that the religious leaders left one by one beginning with the oldest. There is the potential implication that this was also the wisest person who realized the subtleties and implications of the message of Jesus on lust and adultery. They were doing an ancient version of the Amos Tversky test. You may have heard about the reputation of this brilliant man. People were judged by their own intelligence on how quickly they could recognize that Amos Tversky was smarter than they were. So too did the wise see the writing in the dust.

We must not forget our own role in any of the stories of Jesus. We are meant to identify with the characters at some level in the story. Our choices are rather limited here. Perhaps we are the crowd that has come out of curiosity to church to hear some stories, but not necessarily act on them. Of course, we recognize that we have done our own sin like the woman and celebrate that if Jesus can forgive what some would consider an extreme measure then so to can we be forgiven. By the same token, we might do well to consider ourselves as representatives of a faith that sometimes becomes too ensconced in its interpretation and ritual. Accordingly, we might do well to look within ourselves and walk away with a better understanding.

YEAST AND THE BREAD OF LIFE

As unsettling as it may be, we really don't believe that we have many of the original words of Jesus. When a group of scholars spent many years analyzing the various parables and other sayings of Jesus, the one that received the most votes was the very simple parable found in Matthew chapter 13. There we read that the kingdom of Heaven is like leaven that a woman hid in three measures of flour until everything was leavened. In this parable, it is not simply that Jesus employs a common symbol, but rather that he takes a symbol that was often used in a negative sense and presents instead, a striking image that is provocative. Amy Jill Levine illustrates this wonderfully in her book Short Stories by Jesus.

Indeed, as Amy-Jill Levine notes, the yeast or leaven was like comparing something to that which is corrupt and unholy. This is hardly an image of God that we wish to portray most of the time. This characteristic feature for Jesus to turn things on its head, is seen in other parables as well. As is always the case, the context is essential to understand this parable, rather than trying to make it into an allegory as so many sermons do. First, it is important to recognize that this type of leaven referred to by Jesus is what we would call today sourdough starter. Biblical scholars have noted that such leaven was used as a symbol of the unclean or corrupt. The odor that is associated with us before the end product can indeed be repulsive.

The gospel Matthew is indeed, big on the concept of measures related to bread. In the wilderness temptation of Jesus by Satan in Matthew, we read that the first temptation after 40 days of fasting was for Jesus to turn the stones that were present into bread. What Jesus denies for himself through the power of God, he will not deny or others. Just a few chapters later in the sermon on the mount, Jesus will give the Lord's prayer in which he tells people to demand from God their daily bread. This should not be misconstrued as a metaphor, but a rather practical application of providing the essentials for a group of people that was not so well off.

Later on in Matthew chapter 14 following our parable of note, we see that Jesus is going to bless a few small loaves of bread that are present and feed 5000 people by this sharing experience. Jesus may have accepted that it was enough for him to live by the word of God when he was in the wilderness and being tempted to turn stones into bread, but that's such was not enough for the every day person. The gospel of John will culminate from the very practical to the incredibly symbolic bread of life. On one hand, this rich metaphor is very compelling, but on the other hand, too often times people mistake the metaphor, for the very practical gospel of Jesus.

For a practical matter, Jesus audience would have been very familiar with the story of the unleavened bread from the Original Testament. This was indeed a sacred ceremony. We refer to this today as the Passover. This term derives from the Original Testament story when the Jewish people were captive in Egypt and had the blood of the lamb on the door post so that the angel of death would literally pass them over. Jesus own ultimate sacrifice came at the end of his life on earth life when he went to Jerusalem to celebrate the feast of the Passover. This lead to his anticipated capture and death on a cross.

The stories of hospitality in the Original Testament would not have been lost to the Jewish audience of Jesus. Rather they would have called to mind the hospitality of Abraham when he was entertaining angels, and perhaps the Lord himself. There he tells his wife Sarah to get some bread for his guests much as Jesus told his followers to tell God to provide bread in the Lord's Prayer. This story precedes the announcement that Abraham and Sarah in their advanced age will have a child. When we recall the story, we note that Sarah laughs to herself and wonders after she has grown old was she and her husband have pleasure. Although the sanitized interpretation of that is for the pleasure of the forthcoming child, Amy-Jill Levine points out that this statement is very much referring to sexual pleasure.

WOMAN WHY DO YOU CRY?

The gospel of John is full of metaphors for Jesus. The opening verses mention the metaphor of light which is essential for life itself. The light shines in the darkness and the darkness has not overcome it is what we read in chapter 1 of John verses four and five. Jesus also compares himself to a temple in a second chapter of John. The next metaphor comes in chapter 3 of John, where Jesus is talking to Nicodemus about being born again. The physical birth is only a metaphor for the deeper spiritual birth. Jesus goes on to use both wind and water as metaphors.

We are familiar with the bread of life as a metaphor for Jesus, but also food in general is seen as a metaphor in the fourth chapter of John. Jesus is seen as the gate for the sheep, as well as the good Shepherd. Jesus is the way the truth and the life. Jesus is the true vine. Jesus is the resurrection and the life. These are all powerful I am metaphors. Perhaps the metaphor that Jesus is identified most with is I am the way, the truth and the light. Nowhere, though, do we see Jesus referring to himself in this gospel as a gardener or anywhere else in the Scriptures for that matter.

We turn to chapter 20 of the gospel of John to see where Jesus is mistakenly referred to as a gardener. In this chapter, we see that on the first day of the week while it was dark, Mary Magdalene went to the tomb. In this version she is alone, but saw that the stone had been removed from the entrance and ran to tell Simone Peter and presumably John. She makes the charge that they have taken the Lord out of the tomb and we don't know where they have put him without defining who "they" is. Then the two disciples returned to their previous preoccupations, Mary returns to the tomb and stands outside crying.

The Angels by the nature of their question are either sympathetic and trying to probe why Mary is crying or they are putting down Mary for crying and she does not get it. The Angels only asked one question and then are not heard from again. They ask why Mary is crying. Next Mary makes an accusation to the angels, not necessarily one that involves them. She states that they have taken my Lord away, and she does not know where they have put him. Mary turns next to see Jesus, but mistakes him for a gardener. The gardener image of Jesus asked why she is crying and who it is that she is looking for. The Jesus, mistaken for Gardner image, had initially merely repeated what the angels said by asking Mary why she was crying. However, there is an important addition that recognizes the question who is it you are looking for.

Mary presumes that it would be natural for a gardener to carry the body of Jesus away, apparently more so than two angels. This time, though she does not make presumptions, but rather asks the Jesus Gardiner image to tell Mary where they have taken the body and that she will retrieve him. Jesus mentions her name for a reality check. Then Mary has an epiphany and recognizes that it is Jesus whom she refers to as teacher. Now we have settled in on reality. There will be no more metaphors representing Jesus through the end of the gospel of John after this encounter. This is despite the gospel of John being a very rich source of metaphors in general.

Up until this point of Jesus calling Mary by her name, she is bound and determined to retrieve a body that either one person gardener or two angels or the combination of have perhaps displaced the body that she has come to anoint. She will do this by herself. She gives as much that type of statement to the supposed gardener in a non-accusatory fashion. Hearing her name by a familiar teacher was enough to give her a reality check. She is now able to get on with her life and communicate the message of Easter that goes beyond metaphors, even as it deals with the familiar. To be sure Mary is never put down for crying, but only asked to examine herself by both the angels and Jesus as to why.

We can only follow the individual mission for our own life when we are able to remove the upset and tears over circumstances that inconvenience us. Only when we recognize the universal voice as well as inner voice that connects to our purpose and society at the same time, can we truly fulfill our unique mission. Until that time, we search for the metaphor that will move us just as we search for the strength to remove barriers in our life. When our tears and fears are both recognized and put in perspective at the same time, we see more clearly the origins of truth that go beyond metaphor.

The great I AM who created the Garden of Eden and subsequently banished the humans from such residence has returned disguised as a gardener to tell seeking humans that it is futile to seek the living among the dead. The gardener does not take bodies or transform them into angels. Rather he allows himself to be transformed into all that he is capable of. We must alert ourselves as to what word or tone or voice that we use or hear will awaken us to reality.

GENESIS PART 1

WOMEN AND GOD. ENCOUNTERS AND QUESTIONS

You do not need to be a radical feminist to recognize that there is not a lot of positive dialogue from God to women in the Original Testament In fact our initial impression might be just the opposite. Let us confine ourselves to the book of Genesis initially here to get a better handle on the interactions of God with women. Our first encounter is, of course, in the Garden of Eden where Eve has deviated from the plan laid out by God and eaten the forbidden fruit. The subsequent encounter begins with questions from God who if omniscient would already know the answers. There is a second portion to the formula which begins with the male when both male and female are present. God begins by asking where Adam is. When Adam replies that he is hiding as God would already know even if not omniscient, God asks another question to the male only. He wants to know who told him that he was naked. This is followed its the question of if Adam had eaten the forbidden fruit. The man makes a weak effort that implicates both God and the woman by noting that the woman, Eve, that God gave Adam, gave him some fruit and he ate it. It is as though he had not done it to acquire the wisdom of discernment between good and evil unlike the woman had.

After all of this inquiry, God will turn to the woman and begin with a question "what is this that you have done?" The woman then proceeds to blame the serpent. Now that God has done his detective work, he can begin to lay out the penalties. This he does from the seemingly root cause beginning with the serpent, next the woman, and finally, the man. We can debate who gets the harshest sentence, but the man is the only one that God acknowledges had a direct command to avoid the fruit. We need to recognize that it was by implication that the woman heard the command as well as the consequences from Adam rather than from God. Satan has pointed out that literal statement of God that when one eats the forbidden fruit, that they will die is not true. In this regard Satan is correct in that neither the man nor the woman died at the point of consumption. We must introduce figurative speech to keep God's words as true. We can say that what God meant was that if they ate the fruit that someday they would die as opposed to staying naively alive forever. We can say that we believe that God meant that they were at that moment dead to the bliss of the Garden of Eden. The problem with either choice is that we are deciding what God meant even though he did not say either. We have done a substitution that is natural but not literal. In that regard, Satan proves to be right. They do not die WHEN they eat the forbidden fruit.

There are no further God to female conversations until God confronts Hagar when she is fleeing from her owner Sarah in Genesis chapter 16. Once again, the encounter begins with a reminder question-combination. The reminder is that Hagar is the servant to Sarah and by implication should not be fleeing. God had to know that Abraham had allowed Sarah to mistreat Hagar, if not outright beat her. God asks Hagar where she has come from and where she is going. This appears to be more along the line of a parent asking their child "what do you think you are doing?" when they should be doing something else. In the verses that follow, God commands Hagar to return to the same environment in which she was mistreated. There is a rather positive blessing that follows.

All seems to go well for a while with Hagar, Abraham, and company. Hagar delivers a son for Abraham. That son, Ishmael participates in the covenant of circumcision with his father Abraham, at the young age of 13. Sometime later Isaac is born and Sarah perceives that Ishmael was mocking and so she wanted this poor example of a teenager sent away. Once again Abraham goes along with this request in Genesis chapter 21. Once again Hagar flees to the desert. Once again God finds her and begins with questions. He asks the rhetorical question of why she is fleeing. Before she can answer God tells her not to be afraid. He then repeats his pledge of a blessing to the boy and his offspring.

All the dialogue from God to Hagar is basically positive. Contrast this with the very limited dialogue between God and Sarah. That dialogue sandwiched between the above dialogues and is found in chapter 18 of Genesis. Like the creation-Garden of Eden story, God begins his encounter with talking to the male, Abraham. God begins with a question meant for Sarah, but asked to Abraham as to why Sarah laughed when God said that she and Abraham would conceive a child in their extremely advanced age. Sarah speaks to God exactly 4 words before God speaks to her by noting that she did not laugh. God responds with exactly 4 words and says "yes, you did laugh. "There is no additional dialogue or blessing unlike the Hagar instances. We fast forward to the New Testament story where a woman with a bleeding disorder believed that she could be healed by just touching the coat of Jesus. Of note like many people today, she suffered under the care of many doctors and accordingly spent all her money on them according to the account in Mark chapter 5. She indeed proceeds with her plan and is instantly healed. Jesus senses the power exchange and like God begins with a question of who touched him. This question seemingly meant for the crowd to help him is meant only for the woman to come forward. The woman had used a combination of the indirect approach with a direct touch. In so doing she had used some of the very approach that God used to women in Genesis. We can through the questions of Jesus appreciate that divine questions are meant to be penetrating so that our motives and our mission is clear to ourselves. In addition, we see that when we submit to the questions of the Master, that we are given the important gift of being free from our suffering and having peace as is given to the woman who touched his coat.

WHEN GOD ENDORSED BLAME AND CURSED

The early anthropomorphic description of God is that there was enjoyment with human interaction. God appears to be genuinely disturbed when he shows up on earth, and expects to have his usual walking conversation with the human beings. This anthropomorphic god does not seem as omnipotent as later pictured, as somehow that

God has no perception of where the human beings are hiding let alone why they might be hiding.

When we read the story many generations later, we want to pretend that God actually knew all along, but there really is no evidence of that. As to the question of why the human beings were hiding, it might seem obvious that it was because of their guilt from partaking in the forbidden fruit. While that may be true, at some level, it would appear that the root cause is fear which is exactly what Adam says to God when Adam is confronted.

So, we now have Adam and Eve aware of knowledge of good and evil, and yet afraid of the consequences of that awareness. This anthropomorphic God then begins the on-the- spot inquisition, and wants to know if the perceptions of the humans eating the forbidden fruit is correct. Adam immediately blames the woman. The woman in turn blames the serpent. This leaves no one for the serpent to blame.

Adam confesses to his guilt of partaking. Then Eve follows with her own confession. Despite no such confession from the serpent, this anthropomorphic God then proceeds to presume guilt without a trial for the serpent. This is at least an indirect endorsement of assigning blame. This may will have historical significance of great magnitude when people like Hitler invoke a source of blame when things are not going well. Following the assignment of blame, God begins to curse.

The cursing begins in reverse order of the blame game above. First, the serpent is cursed. Closely tied to that is the woman who is cursed. Finally, Adam is cursed. Following all of this cursing God decides to participate with a literal cover-up for what had been a metaphorical cover-up up to that point. The anthropomorphic God determines that the disobedient human beings will now need clothing and proceeds to make the clothing for the humans.

The plurality of God that we have referred to earlier, is once again acknowledged immediately, following the manufacturing of clothing for the human beings. That God notes that the man which appears to refer to humankind with both, Adam and Eve, has become like one of us. We really do not know historically what the term us means, but we suggest that we resist both the tendency and temptation to note that such refers to the Holy Spirit, or Jesus, or any other representative.

When The Sons of God Had Fun And God Was Sorry

Chapter 6 of Genesis has some interesting passages that lead anyone to try to ascertain the interconnection between them all. The chapter starts with an acknowledgment that people are following the earlier commandment of God and being fruitful and multiplying as God instructed them in Genesis 1:28. Maybe God had a purpose in mind behind that multiplying that comes to light in Genesis chapter 6. An issue is made that daughters were born to them.

These daughters were so beautiful that they caught the attention of the sons of God. Those sons then married whichever women they wanted. Immediately we are told that God wants to limit the lifespan of humans although we are not told what the offspring of these sons of God and women marriage arrangements were. They were apparently not the Giants known as the Nephilim. We are told next that the sons of God had offspring with the daughters of humans and then became heroes.

It's not clear what they did to earn their hero status, but it would appear that some of their purpose was to not have humans worry about the giant Mephilim. But neither giants, nor fear of giants, nor the Sons of God, nor their offspring can prevail to keep humans from descending to wickedness. Apparently, these sons of God could be attracted to earthly women while humans only lusted. Indeed, we are told that every human inclination was only evil all the time.

This dereliction impacts God enough that God regrets having made humans. So, God announces the only thing a creator can do under such circumstances which is to wipe out all the human race and along with it all of the measures that were supposed to be under their dominion. Then to make sure that we do not miss the ethos, we are told once again that God regretted having made them. That is except for Noah. God trusts Noah and tells him that God will destroy all men due to excess violence.

We will skip the details of building the ark and the details of entering the ark with the various animals and the flood itself. When Noah comes out of the ark, he receives a command from God that is reminiscent of Genesis 1:28 with the addition that all of God's creatures are to be fruitful and multiply unlike the limited humankind in that first chapter. To be clear God knows that humans are still evil in every inclination but God promises to stop cursing the ground because of them.

The Short Shrift Of Women Of Genesis – Part 1

Imagine that you are an outsider of the Judeo-Christian faith. Would your perspective be that women are treated equally to men? To answer that question, we begin literally at the beginning. In the creation story, we see God clearly portrayed as a male. However, we do not see this male trait given until there is separation and distinction in creation itself. This occurs in verse three of Genesis chapter 1 in which God separates light from darkness and makes the distinction of night and day.

Scholars are appropriate to point out, however then when it comes to creating humans that the language implies that God made male and female at the same time from a common source. Furthermore, we have the statement in Genesis chapter one where God says let US make humankind in OUR image which then describes making men and women. Does the US and OUR refer to a suppressed feminine element. Arguably if both men and women are created in the image of God, then God must have both images contained within.

It is only later versions asserting their limited interpretations that feel compelled to have more distinction than necessary. Following up on this concept for misinterpretation is the hindsight interpretation that the female is more to blame in the encounter with the serpent because she was approached before the male was approached. However, when we look at Genesis chapter 3 that gives the account of interaction with the serpent, the woman indeed corrects the language of the serpent. She then shares the opportunity with her male partner to become like God, in recognizing both knowledge and distinction of good and evil.

Of course, there is more to the story that the anthropomorphic God uncovers when he comes down to earth to have his walk with the humans. Curiously, the humans have hidden from God somehow not because they disobeyed a command from God, but rather because they were naked just as God had made them. They were sensitive about that. Hence, we have come to think of nakedness as something naughty and sinful and attached much of that notion to natural human sexuality and continued to blame the female for such natural instincts.

Arguably The humans are punished because they have tried to cover up their natural primeval state and are sensitive about their nature or their awareness of such. Then we have the curious curses given to the three parties involved in eating the forbidden fruit. The curses are given in reverse order to the uncovering nature of the offense. That is, God first gives the curse to the serpent. Next, he gives a curse to the woman, and finally to the man. we might consider the curse of childbirth pain as nothing more than an anthropomorphic mythological representation. However, when we read the sentence following that we see that women are destined to desire their partners, but that the partners will rule over them, we may come away a bit uneasy. The perpetuation of this process throughout the ages has gone too long in the unquestioned fashion

Between the story of Adam and Eve and later Abraham and Sarah, there is not much information about female action, although they appear in the background. During that stretch, we appear to have a very male God destroying all of the Earth with the exception of a limited remnant directed by Noah and his family. Following that humans make an effort to come together and build a tower that will reach to the heavens so that they might make a name for themselves rather than be scattered. The male God does not like this notion that humans could reach his domain of heaven and has some stated concerns that what humankind would propose to do would not be impossible. In the next verse though we note the reference that God gives to us when he says let US go down and confuse the language. This is potentially the same US of the feminine nature referred to above in the creation. If so the feminine element gets credit for the creative as well as destructive side of God.

The Short Shrift Of Women
Of Genesis – Part 2

Imagine that you come from the type of family that has an uncle who has bargained with God successfully on five occasions and arguably has saved your life. Furthermore, during the rescue mission, your mother became an infamous example in history by merely looking back on what she was leaving, and accordingly was turned into a pillar of salt and died. Perhaps your father might try to shelter you from the exposure to the evil of the society that you were leaving behind. Indeed, this appears to be the case for Lot following the destruction of Sodom and Gomorrah. Lot has asked God to spare a small town perhaps because they did not have as much evil in them in total as did Sodom and Gomorrah. God does just that but Lot decides that it is not in the best interest of him and his daughters to live there.

So, Lot heads for the very mountains that God told him to go to initially, but which he rejected initially. This leaves the family living alone in isolation. In fact, they are living in a cave. The daughters though decide that they want children and that the only way to get such children under the circumstances is to have intercourse with the only male around. Since it is their father, they will have to get him drunk on successive nights in order to do that. Keep in mind that this is the same father who is willing to give the two daughters to the men of Sodom and Gomorrah to have their way with them in order to protect the visitor angels. Perhaps the daughters recalled this very willingness, and did not think much about the drunkenness and incest. This makes us wonder what these sins of Sodom and Gomorrah could have been when drunkenness and incest become part of a story in which offspring are given to the daughters. Interestingly the unions of these incestual relationships seem to be mentioned in positive terms with no evidence of wrong with specific mention of the offspring.

Following this, we will see Abraham on two occasions try to pawn off his wife as merely his sister, which was somewhat a half truth, but certainly one told out of deception to save his own skin. Following that we see that Sarah laughs at God when she is told that she will have children and is chided for such although Abraham seems to get off rather easily under the circumstances. All of this pales in comparison to the story of Hagar, who seems very much misused by Sarah and perhaps Abraham himself. Abraham impregnates Hagar, then sends her to wander in the wilderness at the request of his wife Sarah, who seems a bit jealous. Hagar will serve as a role model first for Joseph in the desert and later for Moses in the desert.

As we have noted in our book on the patriarchs, Hagar is the only person ever in the Bible to rename God. Indeed, it would appear that Hagar is the first human to practice a human-to-human concept of forgiveness. She must indeed forgive both her mistress Sarah, who has abused her in some way, and Abraham, who has at least not stood up for her, but quite possibly taking advantage of her as well. All of this forgiveness predates the forgiveness that Esau experienced when he had his birthright stolen by Jacob. It also very much predates the forgiveness that Joseph had for his brothers after they sold him into slavery. Nonetheless, I have heard people blame indirectly or directly Hagar just because she seems to not be part of the larger promise.

There are not a lot of other leading women in the book on Genesis. One that does not get much attention surprisingly is Rebekah. This is despite the fact that she leaves her home and homeland and goes to a foreign land to marry someone sight unseen. Some times she is seen as participating in the scheme to deprive Esau who was the firstborn of his birthright. However, we must temper that with the fact that God had already promised a larger role for Jacob than Esau. Furthermore, Esau had willingly given up his birthright when he was famished and Jacob made the deal. Rebekah's role was to contribute to the deception for the Blessing which was also reserved for the firstborn.

For the rest of Genesis that leaves Rachel and Leah, the 2 wives of Jacob as the remaining women of stature. Jacob loved Rachel but had to marry Leah to acquire Rachel. Yet it is Leah who is blessed by God. This is countered by the notion that Jacob favored the 2 sons born by Rachel, namely Joseph and Benjamin. Furthermore, we have another story of deception with Rachel who stole the gods of her father and pretended to be having her period when they came looking for the missing gods.

So, all in all we have 2 potential role models for women in Genesis that we seldom hear about. There is Leah who keeps having babies and never seems to mind the fact that her husband Jacob loves his younger sister Rachel more who is said to be more beautiful. Granted she is not pushed aside to the degree that Hagar was, and yet both of these women seem to be ignored in sermons when indeed they not only served a role in making the offspring of Abraham as much as the sand on the beach and stars in the sky, but also as role models for men and women for quietly accepting their status and still managing to forgive the significant slights that they received. The time has come to dissolve the short shrift.

The Creation Of Blame – Part 1

I will have a discussion from time to time with a good friend about what humankind has created, as opposed to the creation by God. For many years, I pointed out that the only humankind invention was that of time. While it is true that God made divisions between day and night, it is only humankind that truly marked time as we think about it today. It is as though it becomes a marker of our distinction from the rest of existence. Paradoxically it is only when we negate time that we are truly existential and living in the Now.

That having been said, we will now give another contender for an invention by humankind. For this we return to Genesis chapter 3 in what has become to known as "the fall". Even the concept of "the fall" implies that humankind had to fall from something. They did not fall from grace, because there had been no extension of grace up until that point. In fact, it would appear rather that there was an ascension to the concept of knowledge rather than that of a fall. We might even call it the kick out chapter because they were kicked out of Paradise.

The chapter begins with the introduction of the serpent. It will take many years before the serpent acquires the name of Satan. This is well detailed in the book the Origins of Satan by Elaine Pagels. The first sentence states that now the serpent was more crafty than any of the wild animals the Lord God had made. We pause to analyze on the word the first word "now" as the serpent creature as being someone in the now. Someone who is aware. Someone who asks questions. There is ambiguity, perhaps by intent, as we reference shortly.

The serpent begins with the question of asking did God forbid all fruit from the trees of the garden. We must keep in mind several implications from the information that we have been given thus far. We are told that all of God's creation is good. Furthermore, it would appear that God has created all creatures, with the option of ambiguity mentioned above. There is however, some ambiguity about that of the serpent. We are not really told that God created the serpent, but rather that the serpent was cleverer than any wild animal God had made.

The woman, whom we identify as Eve, corrects the serpent's statement that they indeed may eat of every tree except for one. She names the tree in the center of the garden correctly, but she adds something to the story and forbidding aspect that God gave in Genesis chapter 2. God did not say to not touch the tree. Therefore, we are left with the choice that God actually said it, but it was not recorded. The next choice is that Adam added this for which we have no record. That leaves us with the notion that Eve added this embellishment.

Now we have the serpent, pointing out that in advance that God was lying. He says to the woman that they will not certainly die if they eat the fruit. Rather their eyes will be opened for the distinction of good and evil. No matter how much fundamentalists wish to distort what is actually written as to being figurative, they must introduce the concept of something that goes against the literal recorded word. After all, the humans do not die in the literal sense. Not in the moment of Now that the King James Version says in that very moment of ingestion

THE ANGEL OF THE LORD

The appearance of the angel of the Lord from the Original Testament forward, signifies a rather important happening. After all, the angel of the Lord does not appear to just anyone. Although there are not a lot of visits from the angel of the Lord to men in the Original Testament, there are only two visits by the angel of the Lord to women. The first occurs in Genesis, where Abraham has impregnated his slave mistress Hagar at the insistence of his barren wife Sarah. We recall that Sarah was unable to bear children, but knew how much Abraham wanted and needed an heir and decided to step in.

Already by this time, Abraham had been promised that he would have heirs as great as the stars in the sky, the sand and the dust. That promise came from no less than God. However, if God had not delivered on the promise, and our spouse was old and well beyond childbearing age, we might not be surprised at the response of any man who was told by such an aged wife to have sex with a younger woman in order to fulfill the promise that God had not delivered on. We have detailed the story of Hagar elsewhere, including our book on the Patriarchs.

The only other time that the angel of the Lord appears to a female in the Original Testament is to an unnamed woman. To be sure we have something about her identity in that she is the wife of Manoah. Perhaps more notably, she becomes the mother of Samson, who is reportedly the strongest person ever to have lived. When we ask people to recount what they can about Samson, they will, of course remember his great strength. A second measure that they can usually recall is that he was deceived by a woman who cut his hair which led to the loss of that great strength. Never mind for the time being that that great strength is restored by God through request by Samson when he will use that strength to kill a number of his enemies, along with himself.

What seems to be missing so often with the retailing of these stories is that we seldom have much made of the fact that an angel of the Lord appeared to these females who had great roles. In the case of Hagar, we have the slave mistress who was a foreign woman of color who appears at some level to have been abused by Sarah wife of Abraham. To a fair degree a case can be made that Abraham himself abused her and then abandoned her. Her death would have been eminent upon such abandonment if she had not been rescued by God in the desert. During that ordeal she becomes the only person recorded in all of the Bible male or female to rename God.

The mother of Samson represents all women who are unnamed play a significant role in bringing strength into this world, even when they are unnamed. These types of appearances set the stage for the New Testament appearance by the angel of the Lord, named Gabriel to the lowly Mary, wife of Joseph and eventual mother of Jesus. Unlike the role of Gabriel in the Original Testament where his role is that of connection with apocalyptic end times, in the New Testament Gabriel will be linked with the new age of salvation to all of people everywhere, including the poor and children and outcasts. This is the message of the universal Gospel as opposed to a sectional and sectarian and male dominated religion.

To be sure, upon hearing the news that Mary will become the mother of someone who is to become a savior, she is troubled by those words. She responds how can this be. She is, after all, from a very humble background. Accordingly, we are told that Mary ponders on these measures. Yet she also treasured the story and in particular the words of Simeon, as we were told in Luke chapter 2, where she treasured all of these things in her heart. Her perplexity may be compared to Moses in the Original Testament who made protest to God when he was called because he was slow of speech and tone. We see a similar protest with the prophet Jeremiah.

Ultimately Mary calls to mind images of a young woman like Hagar, who is connected to an older man. We do not wish to imply that Joseph used her or abused her in anyway shape or form. Rather when others might have abandoned her due to her pregnant appearance, which was not by his hand, he chose to stay with her unlike Abraham, who is ready to abandon Hagar. What Mary shares with the mother of Samson is having a son who is strong and some in some way that will both threaten other people and leads to his own death for a greater cause.

The Creation Of Blame – Part 2

Some versions try to wiggle out of the immediacy of death after ingestion of the forbidden fruit by implying that this is a future Will die type of process. Again, we must keep in mind though that time has not been invented. We don't even know about eternity. Eugene Petersen does not dodge this concept in his version of the Message when he notes that the moment you eat from the tree, you're dead. The King James preserves the immediacy of death. It is not clear why certain versions felt the need to sanitize and preserve their retrospective theology by vacillating between literalism and figurative depending on what fits their fancy.

Let us return to what is recorded. God is used to walking with the humans in the garden of Eden. One day God comes down and cannot find the humans. Such would appear that God is not omniscient, even though God knows the distinction between good and evil. Now the humans become aware of such a distinction. God asked them why they were hiding. Adam's response is that they were afraid. Why were they afraid? They were afraid because they were naked and so they hid.

The human beings have indeed transitioned from having nothing to hide to the literal cover-up, which perhaps serves for eternity as the ongoing and perpetual metaphorical cover-up. This is the cover up of distinction from the Other. This includes the progression of the distinction between men and women. The best scholars have pointed out that the language of creation implies that God made humans out of one body. That is that Adam and Eve as we call them, were once united in body and then separated. The language referencing is the plural "us". We moderns have reversed the order of God as plural and humans as united.

Following the ingestion of the forbidden fruit of good and evil, they become aware of the fear of the separation of the ego. They become more aware of the distinctions of the Other, as well as the distinctions from the rest of the creation of God. With this recognition of separateness or otherness from creation, they have effectively thrown themselves out of the garden. We indeed have a hard time of blaming God for the expulsion. That leaves us with the choice of blaming humans themselves or the serpent.

Adam precedes to make the first human confession. It is a confession that does not appear to be followed by forgiveness. It is a confession with the introduction of blame. To be clear, the blame that Adam proposes is somewhat ambiguous. We can interpret his statement as blaming God because after all, God gave him the creation of female. Our alternative is to blame himself , which is what we tend to do in hindsight since after all, we have so much more knowledge than those primitive people . We have confused knowledge for otherness.

Now it is Eve's turn for blame. She precedes to blame the serpent. When it comes time for the serpent, there is no one left to blame. God precedes to curse the characters involved in reverse order. He curses the serpent first. Then God curses the woman Eve next. Finally, he curses the male Adam. In the original introduction of blame, the serpent is the end of the line and not the beginning. Modern churches have reversed the order and begin blame with the serpent which has evolved into Satan. Accordingly, in order to get back into Paradise, we can only take ownership of blame beginning with ourselves.

THE SISTER

If you were going to marry your sister or were already married to her, when would you tell people? When would you tell people to whom it might really matter? When would you have your biographer tell people? Let's look to see what Abraham did and then speculate why. First let's chronicle all the chances that might have been passed up to convey this potentially import6ante relationship. We first meet Sarah in Genesis Chapter 11 under the name of Sarai. The only relationship we are told there, is that she is Abraham's wife. We are not told that she is also his sister. Now most people might agree that a wife trumps a sister, but if you are both then you also note that. Furthermore, her relationship to her own father is not mentioned except as a daughter-in-law. Now we might take some exception and note that probably the relationship of a daughter is more important than that of a daughter-in-law, but certainly as important. And absolutely noteworthy.

Next, we have the first encounter with Pharaoh. The stage is that during a time of famine Abraham journeys to Egypt where food is more abundant. Concerned that Sarah is attractive and that accordingly the man of great faith will be killed in order for such to have access to Sarah, Abraham instructs her to say that she is his sister. Apparently, she does this with great consequences to pharaoh and so is called out on this. Even so if you read the account, Abraham never actually acknowledged that she was his sister or even that he told her to say so. A few key events happen including the announcement that Sarah will actually become pregnant and produce offspring. Then we have the interruption of Sodom and Gomorrah. As despicable as that region must have been, the story of Lot ends with him escaping only to be made drunk by his daughters so that they may have intimacy with him in order to keep the family line going. In the next chapter we once again have Abraham on the move into a new territory with the request once again that Sarah emphasize that she is his sister without reference to being his wife. The ruse is revealed to the unsuspecting by no less than God himself. This time Abraham explains that it was of course to save his life. For the first time he acknowledges to another human being that she is both wife and sister.

Now most of us might think anachronistically that we would never have that type of relationship. But if we did could we pick a better time to reveal such arrangement than after another close relative has intimacy with a first degree relative in the context of the destruction of a very wicked city. The only thing we could possibly seal the deal with is to bring God into the equation in order to provide consequences for authority figures who might not like the arrangement.

GENESIS PART 2

SAME FATHER

Abraham is often referred to in literature and song as Father Abraham. He comes with this title quite reasonably as almost God given. Did not God say to him that he would make him the father of many people? More than the stars or sands, etc. Christians would like to note that they with Abraham serve the same Father in heaven. These platitudes may be comforting to most of us as we look at the universal nature of God's Love. The concept of "same father" has additional meaning for Abraham, though.

When Abraham fears for his life, he tries to pawn his wife off as his sister. He is up front with his wife about the duplicity. He feels apparently rightly so, that others, no less than kings will see her as attractive and want to have her for themselves. He feels then that those same people will look favorably upon him, which is to say, not kill him. He gets most of this right. Even God comes into the arrangement by causing or threatening health compromises to the unwitting suitors. When they call Abraham out on this, he in part confesses. But he also rationalizes. He notes that he spoke the truth because he and Sarah have the same father. Amazingly he repeats this ruse a second time with essentially the same results. Also, God plays a bailout role again. Another scenario can be drawn up because Isaac and Ishmael have the same father in Abraham. Of course, they both go through ordeals one way or another on account of Abraham. We have detailed these elsewhere. The reader can decide who experienced the greater challenge of being a son of Abraham. There does seem to be some comfort in that both boys helped to bury their father, even though

Ishmael had to know that he was not getting anything materially out of the preordained will.

Laughter

Most of us can probably recall vaguely the story of Abraham and Sarah being told that she will conceive a child in her old age after she has been barren for so many years. In fact, while she is 10 years younger than her husband Abraham, she would still be 90 at the time of delivery. Of course, Abraham by that time would be 100. When Abraham is told the news he himself is incredulous. He begins to laugh even as he falls to the ground. He may not have literally fallen to the ground laughing, but all versions are clear in that he bowed down to the ground and was laughing to himself about this preposterous idea. He wonders out loud if a man can have a child at age 100 or his wife can have one at age 90. To add to his doubt, he asks God why Ishmael cannot be his heir. God then proceeds to name the unborn son Isaac which we are told means laughter. All this precedes the scene in the next chapter where Sarah laughs at the same notion. Furthermore the original awareness to Abraham comes in the proceeding covenant chapter. There is first a covenant drawn up between God and Abraham which will be represented by circumcision. Then there is the revelation of the unborn son which represents God's end of the bargain. This is in turn followed by the actual rite of circumcision to all the males in Abraham's household. You could say therefore that this is no laughing matter. But there you have it right smack in the middle that Abraham is indeed laughing.

It is almost anticlimactic that Sarah laughs when she hears the news in the next chapter. What is the difference between her laughter and Abraham's? Both, after all, laughed to themselves. First she picked up her awareness to some degree by eavesdropping as opposed to direct revelation like Abraham. Secondly, she denied the fact that she laughed. She is called out on this and God reminds her that nothing is impossible to HIM. After the destruction of Sodom and Gomorrah and a few other side stories, Isaac is finally born. Sarah suggests that God has brought her laughter (which once again is the meaning of Isaac). Furthermore, she suggests that everyone who knows her and hears the story will laugh with her. Maybe God needed a good laugh after the destruction of Sodom and Gomorrah.

SARAH'S LEGACY

What is the image that most of us have of Sarah? At best it is likely that we view her as a passive partner to a great patriarch. Perhaps we even recall how she laughed when she was nearly 90 and was given a divine message that even though she was barren and advanced in age that she was still going to conceive and have a child. We might further recall that Abraham laughed first but did not lie about the laughter as Sarah did. He also did not get rebuked for it. We probably don't envision this woman as the person who saved her husband's life on two separate occasions. But that is what she did. Let's back up a bit though to her origins and some of the thought as to how she might have been relegated to relative obscurity. We see from the first chapter of awareness about Abraham, namely Genesis 11, that Sarah is also mentioned. But she seems right off the bat to get second billing. We say this in that Abraham's brother's wife is given some background linage whereas Sarah has none. Only the potentially derisive mention that she was barren.

This seems a little strange because later we learn that she is Abraham's sister or at least half-sister. Abraham himself mentions later that he shared the same father with his wife Sarah. So, we have Abraham's brother's wife given her father's linage, but none for Sarah. We must probe why this is so as it seems a little peculiar given the stature of her husband. Was this because Abraham was ashamed that he had married his sister? Was it because Sarah was barren at that time suggesting that just as her line was going to vanish, so too did she come out of nowhere? Was it because she was strikingly beautiful so that everyone knew her background just as men would enquire about a beautiful woman today.

Abraham appeared both impressed by her beauty and fearful of it as well. He may have been so enamored with her beauty, inner and outer, such that he did not mind any consideration about marrying his sister. In the next chapter he suggests to Sarah that she pass herself off as only his sister. The setting is in Egypt where they have journeyed due to a famine in their area. Abraham predicts that the Egyptians will want to kill him when they find out she is his wife, and not merely a sister. He may be right about her beauty and that others including royalty will recognize her beauty. What he is wrong about is that he will be killed when they find out she is his wife. This scenario in Genesis chapter 12 is repeated essentially in Genesis chapter 20. Keep in mind in the second episode we know that Sarah was over 90 and was still considered attractive by Abraham and others including royalty. When it is all said and done the unwitting admirers of Sarah are ultimately punished for their minimal interactions with Sarah. That having been said in hindsight, an argument can still be made that Abraham believed that Sarah could save his life and arguably she did.

In other instances, Abraham shows his respect for Sarah by staying with her in her barren state. He takes a handmaiden to have a child and heir only at Sarah's request. He allows her to have free reign over that handmaiden and child. She does not appear to put up any fuss when Abraham is challenged by God to sacrifice their only mutual child Isaac. Finally, Abraham goes to some length to provide a decent burial and burial site for her. It is too hard to be dismissive of the role she played in the life of this great patriarch.

A Wife for Isaac

Sarah died when she was 127 years old. This made Isaac 37 at the time of her death. He was unmarried and showing no signs of being eager to do so. Perhaps because he came so late in life for Abraham and Sarah he was doted on and spoiled. We have evidence of that early in his life when Ishmael is playing and Sarah doesn't like his style. He sends that son away to the desert even though technically he is Abraham's first born. God has made it clear that Isaac is the son who will inherit all of Abraham's wealth This is the only human that God is present for in the flesh when he is born.

Abraham gets anxious that he might die before Isaac gets himself a wife. So he sets out to take care of that process. He makes his oldest servant swear that he will find a wife for Isaac from among Abraham's family. This may well have been one of the two servants who took Isaac up the mountain when he was going to be sacrificed while Abraham was being tested. It may even have been the original servant that Abraham thought about leaving all his inheritance to when Abraham had no heirs - though his nephew Lot was alive and had essentially been raised by Abraham. This means traveling some distance back to that environment. Abraham makes him swear that he not take Isaac back to that environment though at the same time that he was not to let him get married to a local Canaanite woman.

It's not clear why Abraham does not want to let Isaac leave the area and go to the father homeland of Mesopotamia. Was he, along with Isaac, still mourning the loss of Sarah? Would it be too much to risk a journey and lose Isaac through such a journey? Was he afraid that Isaac might have been lured to stay in that land that had many attractions besides just beautiful women? Was Isaac still a home body? We appear to get that answer later in the chapter when we learn that Isaac had moved to the land of Negev. We will never know no matter how much we speculate what the reason was.

Abraham will journey up the mountain trusting God since there are no people around but will not trust Isaac to come back if there is a woman involved. His matriarch is ideal, Sarah, but he does not trust his son to find the ideal matriarch.

A whole chapter is devoted to this ordeal with lengthy portions told twice. We rely on that faithful servant for the details. Isaac basically does not appear until the end of the chapter, just in time to meet Rebekah and get married. How is that union symbolized? By taking her into the tent of his deceased mother. Then is the first mention that he is comforted after that death. While Abraham can die in peace now as he does in the next chapter, he himself takes another wife after Sarah's death and actually lives another 48 years after her death. Also, that apparent difficulty he had in his old age of Sarah for a child before he sired Isaac was apparently taken care of as he had 6 sons through this second wife. Quite possibly he was more relaxed after he knew his true line of inheritance was going to be fruitful and multiply.

JACOBS'S WIVES

Of Jacob's two main wives, whom did he love the most? At first glance this seems incredibly straight forward. From the time he met them both he seemed to favor the younger sister Rachel. He found her more esthetically appealing by all the descriptions. We all know the story of his willingness to work 7 years for her only to feel swindled when the older and less attractive sister Leah is substituted. We may be down on their father Laban for the substitution but we must examine the story in its entirety for various implications. The young and hormonally stricken Jacob believes he is in love and makes his offer to the father Laban to work 7 years. Read his response carefully. In no version does Laban agree to the arrangement. So time passes quickly and Jacob feels naturally that he has fulfilled his duties for his prize. When Laban substitutes Leah, Jacob cries foul. Laban points out the common custom for many cultures which was to marry off the older daughter first. Then knowing that he had offered to work 7 years once for a woman this time Laban initiates the arrangement. Now regardless of what we may think of Laban he seems to want only a reasonable stake for his oldest daughter Leah. He asks Jacob to spend the honeymoon period of one week with Leah before he will have access to Rachel. Despite the common belief that he must work 7 more years to get Rachel, he actually marries Rachel after that one week and then has relations with her. It's all right there in Genesis 29. Isaac actually is married after the 7years servitude. Laban actually trusts him big time that he will complete the additional 7 years.

To be sure the Lord notices that Leah is not being loved. Accordingly, he opens her womb to bear children. After her third son she prophecies that her husband will become attached to her. After the 4th, she praises God. Naturally Rachel becomes jealous and says to Jacob "give me children or I will die" Genesis 30.1 Now it is Jacob's turn to be angry. He responds "Am I in the place of God, who has kept you from having children?" As per family and cultural tradition, Rachel gives her maid to Jacob to bear children and she delivers literally. Leah has a few more sons and finally Rachel conceives and has Joseph. Shortly after she delivers Jacob makes a request to return to his home as though he now had everything, he needed with Rachel now happy. Of course, Laban still doesn't want him to leave. They have a temporary arrangement but the success of Jacob instills jealousy in the servants of Laban. Jacob flees. He is tracked down. He seems to acknowledge the legitimacy of Jacob leaving with the family, wealth, etc. Alas what he cannot tolerate is that someone has stolen his gods. Turns out to be Rachel who does a great cover-up pretending to be on her period. She never is discovered. Or is she?

In chapter 35 of Genesis Jacob is called upon by God to build an altar. He figures this needs to be a process of total commitment by all his household, servants etc. They are to purge all their foreign gods which Jacob knows them to have. Did he know the story of Rachel's earlier theft? Well, someone had to record that deed who was witness. No sooner is the altar built then Rachel delivers her second and dies in childbirth. While Rachel is buried nearby it is ultimately Leah who is buried with her partner Jacob in the same tomb that Abraham and Isaac are buried with their partners. Certainly, a case can be made that just as prophesied by Leah herself, so too did Jacob in his mature state come to love her more. Keep in mind as we will see later that while Jacob indeed did love Joseph more than any of his other sons, that it had nothing to do with Rachel. We are told that it was only because he was born in Jacob's advanced age. Perhaps more mature than his younger more hormonal self and able to see some things that he could not at an earlier age.

Rebekah's Wishes

Most of us have heard the phrase be careful what you wish for as you might end up getting it. The implications are that we might not really like the consequences. Perhaps it is sometimes that we wish without applying any other effort and therefore don't have foundation to our desires. Perhaps the frustration comes because we did not consult God on the matter. Perhaps we did not ask for enough but with our limited understanding and limited belief system we held our wishes back.

In the Genesis account we have the story of Rebekah which provides some interesting twists. We have recalled the story elsewhere of her being sought out and discovered by Abraham's faithful servant and then taken back to be the wife of Isaac. Was this account in Genesis chapter 24 her first wish. "if this is the way it's going to be, why go on living"? The Living Bible has her saying I can't endure this. God gives her an explanation that there are twins who will be respective progenitors of separate nations. Furthermore, the older will serve the younger. We are never told that her pain is relieved. As much as we would like to think that either God relieved her pain, or that such news and pregnancy status relieved it, or that she was more blessed because she endured, the pain we don't really know. But we may have some clues in he later interactions.

We do know that she favored the younger twin Jacob while her husband Isaac favored the older Esau. Accordingly, she sought to step in for God's promise and deceive her husband in order to obtain the big blessing for Jacob. Perhaps she had already been told that Esau had sold the birthright for food and was simply following through with that plan. We have detailed the deceit of that event elsewhere between mother and son that was perpetrated on an aging father who was blind. Bottom line, her favorite Jacob gets the birthright. In the same chapter that she seemingly gets her wish, she makes the statement that she would rather be dead than to have her son marry one of the local gals. This sounds reminiscent of her statements in pregnancy.

Here is the irony of that statement. It is the last words that she ever utters. There is very little reference to her following that. In fact of the three great patriarchs and their wives, she is actually the only one whose death is not recorded. Be careful what you wish, if it does not involve God.

Did Rebekah love Esau?

We know that Rebekah favored Jacob heavily. That is not hidden on us arguably before he was born. This stems from God telling her that she will have twins and that the older Esau will serve the younger Jacob. Keep in mind that this is one of the few and earliest times in the Bible that we have God speaking to a woman in positive prophetic terms. There is also mention that one will be stronger than the other but we really don't have any evidence that Jacob was stronger than Esau. In fact, in most twin studies the older has more significant physical characteristics. In addition, we know that Esau was a hairy hunter. Jacob meanwhile shows no evidence that he was ever a hunter though he appears to have known how to make very savory dishes. In fact, Esau sold his birthright over one of those dishes. Nonetheless when it comes time to deceive dad for the blessing, Rebekah not only orchestrates the deceit, but also takes the trouble to make the food so it is just the way Isaac likes it. We already know that Isaac favors Esau including his wild game and wants to give him a blessing. Rebekah gets wind of this and does the intervening above. Nowhere do we have any evidence that she despised Esau. In fact, she may simply have been acting out of her belief that God had ordained such but that he might need a little earthly assistance. After Jacob obtains the blessing by deception, Rebekah hears a threat from Esau that he wants to kill Jacob. Rebekah understands the gravity of the situation and sends him away to her family of origin. She makes the remark to Jacob that he can come back after Esau forgets about the whole process, implying that such is inevitable. Then she remarks that why should she lose two sons. By this she means that Esau would kill Jacob and then presumably be banned as per the story of Cain and Abel.

Chapter 27 closes with the statement by Rebekah that she is tired of all these foreign women and no sooner than Isaac sends Jacob away to find a wife in his mother's native land. Did Isaac have this design all along? Did he simply cater to his wife's requests that readily? Does he feel that such is ordained by God? We can only speculate. What we can say for certain is that the first woman that God speaks to in consistently positive language, never shows any direct evidence of hating Esau and arguably protects his life.

JOSEPH, WOMEN, AND THE ECONOMY OF THE ORIGINAL TESTAMENT.

In an age where meaning mattered more than facts and myth was an important source of truth and meaning, we may wonder why details that seem very extraneous creep in to the Bible, especially in the Old Testament. The economy of the available rate limiting elements of writing utensils and devices particularly papyrus would seem to suggest that there would be no room for wasted space. We need to check ourselves then when we find ourselves tending to gloss over certain passages because they don't seem to have any immediate connection to our main event. Here we are not talking about the anachronistic notion of long lists of genealogies which appear in the Genesis account.

Rather, we are talking about a series of stories that seem somewhat tangential and certainly are rarely preached or written about accept perhaps to connect them with bad character.

Let us look a little more closely at several of these obscure space takers and see how they perhaps might come together in the person of Joseph. The first story we will consider is that of Dinah in Genesis chapter 34. Lest we consider that the women who were not wives were unimportant, we are told about the rape of one of Jacob's daughters. Word comes to Jacob apparently through the social media of his time because we do not have any revelation from God to the man who has encountered God elsewhere and been spoken to by him and through dreams. Rather he keeps quiet about it until the violator's father comes to Jacob himself seeking the permission to now have the son do the right thing and marry the girl.

Now the sons of Jacob find out the story following this disclosure and are enraged. Hamor, the father of the perpetrator, suggests to Jacob that the marriage be recognized which will lead to other relationships, both marital and commercial. The brothers seem to go along with this on the condition that the other men are all to be circumcised. Here we are told they readily go along with this requirement. However, they do so not because they have made a commitment to The God of Abraham, Isaac, and Jacob, but rather because they desire the wealth, they perceive will flow their way by such an arrangement given all the blessings that Jacob and his connections have. Whether because of this pretense or because of the classic motif of vengeance, all the men connected with the city and crime are murdered. Jacob is disturbed about this. His disturbance though seems to be more about the fear of retaliation than about the legitimacy of the payback given that the seemingly last word in the event is from the 2 sons of his, Levi and Simeon who say "should he have treated our sister like a prostitute?" Genesis 34:31 (NIV)

The next story which leaves more hanging out there is found in Genesis 35:32. Seemingly out of nowhere the first born of Jacob, Reuben, sleeps with his father's concubine, Bilhah. We recall that Bilhah was the maid servant of Rachel who was the wife of Jacob. When Rachel is unable to conceive, she gives Bilhah to Jacob much as Sarah had done for Abraham earlier. She produces children and all seems good. The older sister of Rachel, Leah, seems to have stopped having children and tries the same ploy as her sister by giving her own maid servant to Jacob for even more children. Reuben then enters the picture by bringing home some mandrakes to his mother Leah, which Rachel desires. Leah trades them for conjugal rights to Jacob which leads to even more children. After a couple of more sons, she produces the Dinah mentioned above. Following this we are told that God finally remembered Rachel and opened her womb to produce Joseph.

Now we return to chapter 35 where Reuben sleeps with Bilhah, his father's concubine as well as his aunt's servant woman. All this is economized in one verse. Now granted we have acknowledged the necessary economy given the limited resources, but this seems incredibly economical. Those who know the rest of the story see that this folly is recognized with retribution to Reuben when Jacob gives blessings to his sons at the end of his life in Genesis chapter 49. His blessing is limited for Reuben because of that violation. The first portion of this event is compacted into 2 verses. Joseph's mother Rachel dies. Then her servant girl who probably raised Joseph to a fair degree and serves in the aftermath of his mother's death, as a surrogate mother appears. It is no wonder that Joseph did not suffer nightmares as opposed to experiencing dreams, or did nightmares about real events allow him to foresee other events that averted other nightmares.

What remains unanswered is who told Jacob about the deed. We take some great liberty here and note that the bluntness of the description may well have been more than the economy of resources. It is consistent with the bluntness and telltale nature of Reuben's younger brother Joseph.

Joseph, Women Economy Part 2

The perceptive reader will alertly note that the challenge to our theory here is that if Joseph was the tattle tale, then why would Reuben have been the only brother who tried to rescue Joseph when the other brothers wanted to kill him? Why would he not foresee that he was going to lose a fair share of his inheritance, whether or not he could envision this going to Joseph? To this we respond that quite conceivably that the man of bluntness, Joseph, simply reported on a violation of customs in his characteristic unemotional fashion. Jacob who has been wronged through this transaction then sees that the child of his wife who owns the concubine does not seem emotionally troubled by this. He therefore softens the consequences substantially and delays them significantly as well. Keep in mind that at the time of the event that Joseph had lost his mother Rachel. This may well have strengthened the need for Joseph to have a mother like resource that he could turn to, namely Bilhah herself who as the servant of Rachel probably had helped substantially to raise Joseph and was going to play even more of that role for a late bloomer whose blunted emotional system paradoxically needed more of that prolonged bond than other children. Ask any mother with Asperger's adult children about this and they will agree in a heartbeat. The ultimate deprivation of full inheritance to Reuben may well be a clear example that forgiveness can happen for extreme behavior but that there will still be significant consequences.

That leaves us with another challenge of how to explain the strange behavior of Judah, another brother, in Genesis chapter 38. There Judah marries a Canaanite woman who produces sons for Judah. One of those sons marries but dies before children are born at the hand of God due to wickedness. Despite the wickedness though there was a duty by his brother to produce children through the widow for those children to receive their own birthright as though they were the brother's own. One brother has repeated intercourse but purposely spills his semen on the ground to avoid pregnancy and producing offspring that would not be legally his. This sexual interaction without consequences is intolerable to God who then puts him to death. Judah then pledges to the widow Tamar that the remaining brother, Shelah, will fulfill those family duties after the age of maturity. We are told though that while Shelah does mature, that Judah withholds him from Tamar. Meanwhile, Judah's own wife dies. Tamar who is tired of waiting disguised herself as a prostitute and gets the attention of Judah who offers gifts for sleeping with the unwitting Judah. Three months later, Tamar is discovered as pregnant and with the double standard of the time, is condemned to be burned to death. Her life and the twins inside her is spared when she reveals Judah as the father by noting the gifts he gave her. What are the consequences to him for these actions? Nothing. Absolutely nothing. Instead, Judah will receive a huge blessing from Jacob that in many ways is bigger than the one for Joseph. Now we might be satisfied that Judah also played a role in saving Joseph from death when he convinced the brothers to sell him into slavery as opposed to killing him like the brothers proposed. That would be tidy and convenient. It could be further supported by the notion that Judah acknowledged his wrongdoing where it is not clear that Reuben ever did. Indirect acceptance of the consequences by either the Genesis historian or God or both is given in the genealogy in Genesis chapter 46. There the offspring of Jacob is listed. Only Judah has 3 generations. Furthermore that 3rd generation comes through the son Perez who was the product of the relationship with his daughter in law.

Ah yes, but....... but what does that have to do with Joseph? Why does he have to suffer through the lies of a woman who Joseph avoids only to be falsely accused and thrown into prison. Consider the possibility that Joseph must endure false accusations by a woman, which indirectly elevates that status and power of women. At the same time it is an opportunity for Joseph to do atonement for all those women listed who have been wronged at the hands of men. Remember the economy of the stories.

Finally, we conclude that Joseph must do atonement for his own mother Rachel who stole the gods of her father Laban when she fled from him with Joseph and then lied about it. She was never discovered. At least by Laban. But perhaps Joseph had become familiar with the story. He knew atonement ultimately had to be made. Enter the hidden cup in Benjamin's sack analogous to the gods hidden by Rachel. This cup will be discovered not only to promote forgiveness to his brothers after a trial to them, but also for atonement for his mother's actions long ago.

We must not lose sight of the multiple potential implications and meanings even amidst the economy of Genesis. The God who knows no limits should not have them imposed by our limited ways of thinking. Do keep in mind that the offspring of Joseph come via the daughter of a foreign priest.

OTHER ORIGINAL TESTAMENT

HOLY MOSES: WOMEN WHO DISOBEYED

Imagine that you belong to a group of people who are foreigners and are unpopular because you may be displacing the local people from some of the material measures that they enjoy. Your own people after all are becoming numerous and apparently taking over various measures. When the king of the country recognizes this fact, he seeks to oppress you and your people. However, the oppression backfires and your people multiply even more so. So, what is a king to do under those circumstances?

If you chose genocide, then you have guessed correctly. To be clear though it is not a complete genocide, but rather directed against the males only. Now it does not only the king who wishes to oppress you, but the entire people of the country are in dread of your ability to multiply and take over. The king therefore, issues a strong edict to the midwives of the Hebrews. We have the names of two who may have been the only two namely, Shiphrah and Puah. They have been instructed by the king in person to kill a male baby at birth, but allow females to live.

It turns out, though that these midwives fear God more than they fear the king, and apparently more than they fear for their lives. They are summoned before the king and questioned as to why they are letting the male babies live. With her own lives on the line, they determined to lie about the event. They note that the Hebrew women are so vigorous that they are delivered before the midwives can arrive. God extended his kindness to the midwives, and the Hebrew people multiplied even more so.

The king had to devise a plan another plan. This time he involved his own people noting that if they saw a male baby, they were throwing it into the Nile River. These are the circumstances that Moses was born under. He was hidden for three months, but following this was placed in a basket into the Nile river while his family looked on. The king's own daughter happened to come by and see the baby crying and felt sorry for him. She recognized that it was one of the Hebrew babies. She chose to rescue the baby and actually employed the mother of Moses to help raise the baby and nurse the baby. It was actually the King's daughter who gave Moses his name.

This process allows Moses to be raised initially in his own home by his own family. This includes the values of his people. However, we are told that when he became older that his family took him to live with the king's daughter. This sounds like a voluntary effort. We maintain as we have elsewhere with Jacob and Ishmael that this was at the age of around 13. This would make him in the hormonal phase of life. Put yourself in the sandals of Moses. You have a charmed life since you were saved as a baby. Then just as you are getting ready to begin the life of a slave, your hormones kick in and you have everything that a teenager could want.

If you were Moses, you might believe that you were invulnerable. You might believe that you have a mandate to save your people from oppression. Here is the problem when you get ahead of the story and you get ahead of God. So, with this in mind the very next thing we see with Moses is that he commits a murder to an Egyptian while defending a fellow Hebrew who was being beaten. Interestingly his fellow Hebrews resents what this privileged boy was trying to do. Therefore, Moses goes into seclusion. So, Moses begins his life in hiding and is rescued by women to belong to 2 nations. Now this murderer is in hiding belonging to neither nation. The women cannot rescue him now. Can God? Only if Moses returns to what the women taught him.

Miriam, Sister Of Moses

Miriam is the older sister of Moses, who saves his life when Moses was a baby. The story is generally well known by most Sunday school teachers, who point out from the scriptures that Pharoah was worried about the Israelites becoming too strong so that he wished to kill all the Israelite male babies by having them thrown into the Nile River. The women for reasons we can only conjecture are allowed to live. This is the world that Moses was born into and for which he was hidden for three months until he could no longer be hidden. Perhaps at that time, it was not merely his size, but the type of crying that he had in potentially crowded conditions not far from where either Egyptians or fellow Israelites who might turn them in.

The mother of Moses determines that it is time somewhat to comply to some degree with the command and edict from the pharaoh. In a sense, she does throw the baby into the Nile River, but throws him in a basket that floats. The older sister is standing nearby. By the fact that elsewhere, we see that there were no other siblings outside of Aaron, this sister is by default Miriam. Some commentators note that she was perhaps only six or seven years of age. There is no basis for this speculation, and so we will post a different conjecture here. We maintain in the economy of telling stories in the Bible that there are comparisons made whenever possible. In this situation, we have the opposite of Sarah and Abraham in which Abraham was definitely older. In our book on the patriarchs, we note that at times by virtue of their age difference that Abraham served as a father figure to Sarah and as the older brother figure before becoming the partner of his half-sister. This, union of blood relatives, by the way, became forbidden in the code God gave to Moses about forbidding such relationships even though this is how the father of the Jewish community began. We therefore see the inversion of turning upside down of both the stories and the law in the story of Moses.

We would suggest that a better model of comparison is that of the age difference between Ishmael and Isaac. This differential may have been closer to 10 years in order to highlight the differences between the two children of Abraham. In fact, we feel that Ishmael came into full recognition as a child of Abraham when he became circumcised around the age of 12 or 13. This thing was the most likely age of decision awareness of Isaac when Abraham climbs the mountain, believing that he is to sacrifice his only true son Isaac to God, which was the same age that Ishmael had to be circumcised. This age of 12 or 13 serves a role in which Miriam is an effective babysitter, but also someone who is approaching the age in the times of potential marriage. She has enough hormone to awaken her female instinct to suggest to no less than the daughter of pharaoh that she can find someone who can breast-feed the baby Moses and take care of him in early life. That person, of course, is no less than her own mother. We do not know if the young princess was married or not, or had had attempts to have children and was unsuccessful. Perhaps she even had her own children already but had compassion on this baby who is fair to behold.

Moses is raised with a dual identity as both Egyptian in the court of the pharaoh, and as a Hebrew by virtue of the family influence. As a young man, the Hebrew influence dominates when he sees an Egyptian quarreling with a fellow Hebrew, and he murders the Egyptian. The following day, Moses attempts to intervene, on behalf of two quarreling Israelites. One of them asks if Moses is going to kill one of them because of such argument, just as he had done the day before. Suddenly Moses realizes that even though he has lived a life in secret that the truth is out. His own life takes priority over justice for his own race. He fleas the situation before he will have his rise to power. We must not forget the role that the midwives had indirectly at saving the life of Moses. These women likely were Egyptian and pointed out that the original edict of Pharaoh to kill the Hebrew babies at birth could not be accomplished due to how quickly the Hebrew women delivered.

Let's keep in mind how Moses was raised, and how that may influence him throughout his life. It would appear that Moses is surrounded by the feminine nature and spirit through the early informative part of his life. This included the young princess as well as likely his older sister, Miriam, and the mother of Moses. There is no evidence that the princess who claimed Moses ever married. Therefore, for better or worse, Moses will not necessarily have this male influence in his life. Indeed, there may well have been many other princesses or royal court females who participated in raising Moses. It is only after he abandons this feminine perspective that he commits the aggressive homicide, which process is usually thought of more as a male or testosterone type of energy.

In the meantime, Moses marries a foreign woman which will come back and play a significant role in the story of Miriam. Miriam, meanwhile, rises to the level of a prophet as we are told in the scriptures, being only one of seven women in the Original Testament to have this designation. She also becomes a leader alongside with her brothers Aaron and Moses. She seems to do fine in this role until such time as she and her brother Aaron murmur behind the back of Moses about Moses marrying the foreign woman. This story is found in the book of Numbers in chapter 12. God determines that this would be a good time to call all three of these people together: Moses and Aaron and Miriam. God points out that he communicates to different leaders in different ways. For Miriam and Aaron, he might employ visions and dreams. However, Moses was the only person at that time that God spoke directly to.

The next thing we see in the text is that consequences must be applied. Miriam is stricken with leprosy. She was not the first of the three siblings to contract this very feared disease. Moses himself had already been afflicted with this condition for short term due to some disobedience. His leprosy resolves on the spot. No pun intended. On the other hand, Miriam had to wait for seven days outside of the camp of Israel. The Israelites had to put on pause their journey into the promised land. Commentators seem to be fond of pointing out that this was a consequence of disobedience, and often failed to mention the earlier leprosy for which Moses was afflicted. We would maintain that Moses was recognizing that good people may be found anywhere in an act of inclusion when he married the foreign woman. Miriam and Aaron did not recognize this as an act of inclusion. . As a consequence, Miriam had to be reminded and be treated in a partial sense as she herself had treated the foreign wife of Moses. That is, she became the outcast that she sought for the wife of Moses. Meanwhile, the people of Israel had to suffer as a whole and delay their journey until a very important person could be restored and hold to the community as she was after seven days.

Some commentators note that Miriam suffered, because she disobeyed God. We would do well to take a look at the text and context of the story in the book of Numbers, chapter 12. Several versions point out that both Aaron and Miriam talked about Moses behind his back because he had married a foreign woman. They did know that it was not only through Moses that God spoke. But rather God spoke through both of them as well. God then pointed out that Moses was the meekest person on earth, and was quietly humble. This appears to be a reference to his feminine side on what he was raised. This feminine side, indeed, will go to bat against no less than God, who has a habit of getting angry and threatening to do significant punishment to the Israelites, including killing them. Time and again, Moses, through his feminine nature, will stand up to God on behalf of the Israelites. The problem that we see with the story of Miriam is that she is being someone who is divisive and not inclusive. In this sense, she is raising to a dangerous level, the male energy, which divides and conquer rather than the female energy. After she has had an appropriate time to restore the energy balance, she is unified with the people that she leads along with her two brothers.

Upon her death, she appeared to have a proper burial. Her significance is recognized many years later in the book of Micah. There in chapter 6, where we read about the justice of God and the requirements to serve God, we are told that God gave Moses and Aaron and Miriam to lead the Israelites out of captivity in Egypt. Shortly thereafter we are told in Micah 6:8 that the only requirements that God has to love justice. and mercy and to walk humbly with your God. Miriam is attributed along with Moses as writing a song about success in a battle. Some traditions hold that after her death that she still made an appearance of sorts by being the source behind the water. This was something that was never a shortage of until her death. Then Moses and Aaron and God collaborate on this very male image of a rock, rigid and not easy to move. The feminine energy of water rises to balance this energy and things flow as Miriam did in her life.

Esther

Would you promote your daughter to have a relationship with a man who when in a drunken state, was known to have gotten rid of his last wife simply because she refused to show her beauty off to his drunken friends? Furthermore, would you give this same daughter to this type of drunken individual, if he was selecting his next partner on traits of beauty that the removed partner was also known for? Next, would you promote the same daughter to approach this man knowing that it could cost her life? Would you do so for a man whose life you saved once only to have him threaten you and all your relatives with death later? The answer to this question is assuredly no. Nor did one of our heroes of our story do this either. Rather, one of our heroes chose to do this with his niece whom he had raised as his daughter due to the death of the parents.

We can imagine that the real father of this woman might have said on his death bed to his brother Mordecai to treat this girl as though it was his own daughter. The details are all right there in the book of Esther. We begin the first chapter with the mighty king, who has conquered many lands near and far, as throwing a party for his friends. After they have consumed a fair amount of alcohol, they summon the queen in order to display her beauty that she is known for. She refuses to do so. Of course, the king is troubled by this and calls for his advisors to give him advice. Naturally, they say what all men anywhere would say that if women realize what power they have there would be no end to such an uprising. They recommend dethroning the queen and replacing her.

Although we are not told that our hero Mordecai actually promoted his niece Esther for a candidate replacement, it would appear that he indeed, was a key part of the set up since he worked in the Royal Palace, and knew what the arrangements were. Esther, like the other candidates goes to the preparatory school of beauty and learns all kinds of beauty secrets. She is eventually chosen as the queen. The king is so impressed with her that on several occasions, he will offer her up to half of his kingdom. We may surmise that this was based on something he saw in her above and beyond the beauty, since indeed, the king was already plenty familiar with plenty of beautiful women.

Alas, the king has another favorite, though, who was not a woman, but rather a strong and influential ruler. The king has put this person in charge as second in command. After his promotion, there is a commandment for all of the subjects of the kingdom to worship this individual known as Haman. However, Mordecai, as a Jew believes this to be a violation of the 10 Commandments, and refuses to do so. This enrages Haman, who determines his vengeance on Mordechai by plotting to have him put to death. However, it is not enough that Mordechai suffer death, but that all of his fellow Jews throughout the land be put to death.

The arrogant Haman brags about his promotion and his plans to his wife. A day of genocide is arranged for the Jewish people. This would appear to be a done deal since the king has not only given his permission, but has given his special seal for the deal. That was along with the fact that Haman is second in charge in the kingdom. Haman, however has one major blind spot, and therefore one major obstacle. He does not realize that the beloved queen to whom the king would bestow half of his kingdom to, is also Jewish. This may come back to haunt him.

When Mordecai gets word of the edict, and the evil plan, he sits around in mourning clothes. This attention is ultimately brought to the queen. She summons him and sends him appropriate clothes to wear in the palace. He refuses this request because he wishes to send a larger message. He feels that the only way to do so is to have Esther see him in this predicament and state of mourning. Esther takes her next risk. She indeed goes to Mordecai to hear what the problem is. Mordecai reasonably warns Esther that the edict must ultimately apply to herself as well, even though she is the queen. This is because ultimately, she was a Jew first. He basically tells her that she must put herself in harms way , in order for her to save the life of her fellow Jews, but also of her own.

After she makes some minor protest noting that anyone who goes to the king without being summoned, could be put in death, she realizes that death may be inevitable for her and many others. After all, Mordecai raises the rhetorical question if perhaps it was not for this moment that God brought her to that particular position. So Esther goes into prayer and fasting for three days while she meditates on a plan to indeed approach the king. The significance of this risk cannot be overstated. Besides what she knows as a potential penalty of death for approaching the king without being summoned, she is also not approaching the king with the full year of preparation of beauty school before she was chosen as queen.

Even the most beautiful person might lose a fair amount of their vitality and beauty, when they are fasted for three days, and furthermore are full of fear of their own death by their actions. Esther set this aside, and decided to take the risk. She arranges for a meeting with the king and prepares dinner for him in which Haman is invited. This will be the pinnacle of the success of Haman, in which he is invited to a limited engagement exclusively with only the king and queen the next night. Furthermore, a ceremony of honor separate from this has been chosen for Haman by the king himself. Most of us would brag about such details to our partners, which indeed, Haman naturally does.

The next night, the king and queen will dine at an elaborate feast, prepared by queen Esther. Apparently, she learned quite a bit in that year of beauty preparation school above and beyond just looking good. Perhaps even more so before this she learned wisdom from her uncle Mordecai, as she was growing up that she is going to apply in this position. Perhaps she will go above and beyond the loyalty to her uncle, and also realize that she is a person of strong Jewish faith, who may indeed have been placed, as her uncle notes, in a position at just the right time to save her own people as well as herself.

Before we have reached this part of the plot, we have been told that one night during a sleepless night that the king wished to have the royal book of events read to him. There it was dutifully pointed out that Mordecai had saved the king's life in his humble position when he overheard some guards plotting against this king. The king had never rewarded Mordecai for this. Haman was never aware of this event, but rather despises Mordecai for his refusal to bow down before him. It is under these circumstances that the king asks Haman what should the king do to show his pleasure to a man the king most favored. Naturally, Haman thought that this was himself, and he describes an elaborate ceremony of recognition. Imagine the extreme frustration and boiling anger that Haman experienced when he himself had to be selected as the one who ran the ceremony recognizing Mordecai. Indeed, the tables were about to turn even more so for Haman

Meanwhile back at the special dinner for the king, queen, and Haman, the king knows that something is on the mind of Esther, and reminds her that he will give her up to half of his kingdom. Queen Esther then asks the king if he would protect her from an individual who had determined to kill her people as well as herself. The king is flabbergasted as to who that individual might be. It is only then that queen Esther reveals all of her identity. She reveals that she is more than just a pretty face. She reveals that she is more than a loyal daughter, or niece or queen. She is a woman of Jewish persuasion and faith. This will set the stage for one of the greatest turnarounds in which Haman himself will be hung on the very gallows that he has constructed for his perceived enemy Mordecai. The concluding chapter number 10 of this short book illustrates how Mordecai came to be the second in command, and was most honored and revered from that day forward.

Kings And Beautiful Women

The first account that we have of kings and beautiful women occurs in the 12th chapter of Genesis. This is where we will officially meet Abraham, as opposed to a few genealogy measures from the proceeding chapter. To put this in perspective, we are a mere chapter away from the tower of Babel where people conspired to build a tower to the heavens and make a name for themselves. Recall that God was not particularly pleased that people speaking the same language were doing this. The remark was that nothing that they would do would be impossible.

God may indeed have with his partners listed as the vague "us" caused confusion in the language, but God had to know that there would still be some universal appreciation for beauty. Indeed, we note in genesis chapter six that the sons of God saw that daughters of men were beautiful, and even married any of them that they chose. It would appear that the choice was for the male only which precedent apparently carried over for a while. In the same chapter, not long after the remark of the sons of God connecting with the beautiful daughters of men, we see in the next verse that God saw how great men's wickedness on earth had become. The note was that every inclination of the thoughts of the hearts of men was evil all of the time. The process was so prominent that God had regret about ever having created human beings and sought to wipe them out with a flood, which story we have told about Noah.

We hear no more about the sons of God and beautiful women, but we returned to chapter 12 of Genesis in which Abraham and his family experience famine. Preceding the later connection with the Israelites in Egypt, Abraham goes to Egypt to live because of the severe famine. he tells his wife Sarah, that he knows that the Egyptians will see how beautiful that she is and want to kill Abraham for their own sake. He asks her to tell a half-truth that she is his sister in order that he might be spared of his own life. Indeed, the Egyptians do find her to be very beautiful. They take her to the king or pharaoh, who has her in his palace, and for her sake, he treats Abraham well. Abraham gets property and riches on account of this relationship. Then, after he has accumulated a fair amount of wealth, the Lord inflicts disease on pharaoh and his household. This called attention to the ruse of Abraham. The pharaoh gives orders for Abraham and his men to take their possessions, and Sarah included and be gone. We are told immediately following this that Abraham was wealthy following this arrangement, in which he took advantage of his wife and a half truth.

The preceding event happened with an unnamed king or pharaoh. However, the process will essentially be repeated in Genesis chapter 20 with the name king of Gerar. Once again, Abraham has instructed his wife to pose solely as his sister and not reveal her connection or at least full connection to the king. This king also has a dream and warning in the dream and questions Abraham following this as to why he had performed such a deception. This time once again, Abraham gets lots of cattle and sheep, but also gets to stay in the land this time. As if this was not enough for this poor king Abimelech, The son of Abraham, that is Isaac, tries to pull off the same ruse to the same king. Isaac, on the other hand, though has less justification because his beautiful wife is not even a half-sister, like Abraham's wife was to him. At that point when he has called out on the process, Isaac acknowledges the deception. This time, though he does not get direct riches from the king, but is blessed by nature and God when the crops of the land yield great riches for him. The king only later asked him to move because of the great success was impinging on the power of the king himself.

We don't have any similar stories like this about kings desiring other people's beautiful partners until the Israelites get their own kings. Literally, the king of all this process is king David himself. As a dress rehearsal for the Bathsheba incident, King David will end up with Abigail who was the wife of another before she became his wife. We have detailed this along with the story of queen Bathsheba. We do not know much about the beauty of Abigail, but we are told about the beauty of Bathsheba. Indeed, David's desire for beautiful women seemed to follow him all the days of his life until close to the end of his life. It seemed to serve as a marker for how much testosterone, and therefore how much in reality power he had. Recall from our book on David and Michelangelo, how we project that David would not even fight Goliath until he was promised the beautiful daughter of the existing king Saul.

We also note that at the sad end of this mighty warriors life and curator of women, king David appears to die A not so glorious death. This is all right there in First Kings. Chapter 1. There we read that basically David has lost his mojo and was old tired and cold. His advisors brought him a young virgin to take care of him and keep him warm. We are told that despite her beauty, the king did not have any intimacy with her. This was not necessarily the plan or intention it appears of the advisers. However, this word appears to have gotten out and in the very next verse one of David's son at Adonijah has a conference with one of the priests , and there is an uprising or insurrection against David, who has lost his mojo as represented in not having sexual relationships with the most beautiful woman available to him. Nowhere are we told that this was out of respect for Bathsheba. In fact, she only enters the picture somewhat later, when word of the uprising is brought to her, which might lead to displacing her son Solomon from being the rightful king. Queen Bathsheba herself, feels obliged to go to King David and bow down before him. Because the beautiful woman Abishag is right by his side she is effectively bowing down before her, and no doubt, well aware of what her role was have been to restore the mojo of king David.

When queen Bathsheba intervenes, she is able to rescue the kingship for her son, Solomon from the older brother Adonijah. Adonijah knows that his life is at risk. He pleads through an intermediary to have his life spared, despite his plot to take over the kingship after he found out that David had lost his mojo. He makes this plea himself in front of King Solomon. King Solomon notes that his life will be spared if there is no evil found in him in which case he will die. The brother is temporarily off the hook. Alas though the dethroned brother is not yet finished. He goes to Bathsheba, mother of King Solomon, and makes a request that he be able to marry this beautiful woman who called attention to the weakness of the great king David by not being able to perform with her. Bathsheba understands where the brother is going with this, but goes along with it because she knows the likely outcome. The request is to go before King Solomon, which she does. King Solomon sees this as anything but good. If this woman has slept with his father King David, then it is a sign once again, that such a man could displace Solomon himself, just as Absolon tried to show his power when he tried to take over the kingship from David by sleeping with the wives and concubines of David. On the other hand, if David did not actually sleep with her, it also would not be a good sign that look, my father could not get the job done, but I Adonijah can. It is because of this request that Adonijah is put to death. We hear nothing about the beautiful woman from that day forward. Some speculate that she would've shared the same fate.

In an upcoming essay we will look at the risks that some of these women along with Queen Esther.

Women And Risk Taking

From time to time Rich and I like to sit in our local Christian coffee shop and have friendly discussions and debates about measures in the Bible. Sometimes we will pull people passing by to poll them and help us settle the friendly dispute. Such was the case recently, with our discussion about who took the biggest risk in the story of Queen Esther. Was it Esther herself or was her uncle Mordecai. Perhaps another question is would I be writing this essay if the other person did not take my perspective. LOL.

Before we get into further discussion of the risk taking, let us return to some earlier examples where men and women are both involved. In the story of the fall in the garden of Eden, it would appear that both Adam and Eve share equal risk. Both appear very much aware of the forbidden nature of eating the fruit. They are aware of some consequences. It may be difficult for them to judge exactly the extent of those consequences as we have argued elsewhere, but it does appear that the risk was fairly equal.

Moving forward several generations, we come to the story of Abraham and Sarah. Keep in mind as we have mentioned In our Book on the Patriarchs that Abraham likely played many roles to his half sister Sarah. Because of their age difference, first of all the older brother. He then likely was a father figure of sorts for her as we noted there. Finally, of course, he was her partner. We are told that she was a very beautiful woman so much so that Abraham feared losing her to someone else such as nobility.

We find two set stories of Abraham's fear in Genesis. First of all, we have an unnamed king in a land where Abraham is sojourning. He tells his wife Sarah to tell a half lie that she is his sister. Ultimately, the ruse is discovered, and Abraham is sent packing. However, despite the deception to the foreign king, Abraham is given parting gifts of significant nature for his efforts. As if this was not enough, Abraham repeats the ruse once again, several chapters later, this time with a named king. Never mind that this example set the stage for his son Isaac to do the same with his beautiful wife, Rebecca.

Our question in each one of the situations here is who is taking the biggest risk? We will not attempt to apply anachronistic moralism, and suggest that our renowned men of old put their wives at risk for their own sake. After all, we must recognize that given the potential for discovery, as indeed happened in each case, they themselves might have lost their life. Meanwhile, conceivably, their partner might have continued living a life of luxury because of their charm and beauty. By the same token, the women themselves were certainly taking some risks given the circumstances in which they might not have only lost their partner, but been subjected to relationships that they were not interested in. Furthermore, the men involved might've had their way with them and killed them following that.

Let's turn to the story of Queen Esther and Mordecai. Mordecai has raised his niece Esther and recognizes unique measures in her. As we have noted elsewhere, this goes for beyond her extreme beauty. He himself works in the king's court . He may be taking some risk himself by bringing in family to the king, which might be considered a type of bribery arrangement. He takes a major chance when he does not bow down to the wicked prince Haman. Following that he takes a risk when he publicly wears ash and sackcloth as a measure of protest and awareness. He takes additional risk when he refuses the queen's request to come to the palace.

On the other hand, Queen Esther herself, take some risk when she goes to the beauty school of preparation as a potential candidate, by being a potential reject, and accordingly having to be available for other peoples pleasures, but not the rewards of half of the kingdom, as was granted to her ultimately by the king. She takes a major risk when she leaves the palace to confront her uncle Mordecai to find out the nature of his protest. He is after all part of a condemned people. Her background connection with him was not known to many at that point. Next, she takes a risk by going to the king with her petition and request when she was not invited, because such penalty could have included seclusion, and even death. She takes her final risk at the private dinner with the king, and the wicked, Prince Haman, and herself when she reveals her identity and request.

These type of reflections are intriguing and good exercises for our own awareness . There are no easy answers here. Come join us for coffee, fellowship and food and we will reveal the winner. Otherwise continue reading our books.

Righteousness And Women

We read in the Scriptures that no one is righteous. No not one. Jesus himself responded to people calling him a good master with a sense of questioning. He noted that no one was good but God alone. With that in mind, we wish to reference some women who are actually listed as righteous in the Bible. There is exactly one in the Original Testament and one in the New Testament. This is not to say before you take a peek at the answer that there are not examples of many positive female role models. There are indeed, many positive female role models, but only two that fit with references to being righteous.

Now that you have paused mentally, ask yourself as to your recollection of positive women in the Original Testament. We will raise another question. Would you have guessed that one of our references was that of someone who posed as a prostitute, and slept with her father-in-law in that role after she had been married to two of his sons? That likely did not strike you as the proper way of thinking for such an individual to be the only female in the Original Testament to be listed as righteous. However, such is the case of our source in Genesis chapter 38. There we are told of the story of Tamar who married first one son of Judah, and after his death, then another. The first one died through unknown means without bearing a son. By the culture of the times,

BIBLICAL WOMEN AS ENABLERS

another son was assigned to marry the widow. He did so, but when he had intercourse, he withdrew so that he would not spread his seed to this woman. God was not pleased with that action, and arranged for himself to kill the second son.

Over time the father of these two sons known as Judah also loses his wife. He takes a journey in which he encounters Tamar disguised as a prostitute. He has some interest in her, but did not have the immediate resources to pay her. Nonetheless, she performs a service in exchange for his signet and seal, with a pledge to compensate her later. True to his word, he sends his payment to the area where the supposed prostitute performed her service. However, there is no such person to be found. That is because by this time Tamar was not playing that role, which so far as we know, was a one time only measure. As if the story already is not intriguing enough it is about to get better.

People will report to Judah that his daughter-in-law Tamar is pregnant by virtue of prostitution. By the rules of the time Judah pronounces that she must die. It is only at that point that Tamar sends a message back to Judah, that she is pregnant by the man who owns the items that Judah had given her. When Judah finds this out, he declares in verse 26 of Genesis, chapter 38 that she is indeed, more righteous than he is. She goes on to play a role not only in the lineage of the house of Judah, but also is one of four women mentioned in the lineage of Jesus in the New Testament. The significance of these four women has been well detailed in many books, including those by Bishop John Shelby Spong .

For our righteous designation in the New Testament, we return to the gospel of Luke. There the angel visits, Elizabeth and her husband, Zechariah, who is a priest. We are told in verse six of the first chapter, that both of them were righteous in the sight of God, observing the Lord's commands and decrees blamelessly. They were, however, childless. By the time of the visitation by the angel, they were also both old. Not just old but very old. The next thing that we see, is that an angel of the Lord appears to Zachariah during his duties as a priest. The angel told Zachariah to not be afraid, which would be the natural response on seeing an angel during your priestly duty. He is told that his wife will bear a son, and accomplish some great things.

At this point, Zechariah merely asks a question of how this could happen, due to both his age and the age of his wife. Apparently angels of this degree with this type of news, do not like to be questioned, and so Zachariah is silenced until the birth of his child. Whether because she was old or because she just wishes to stay in seclusion or perhaps not worry about being any place that angels might show up and silence her, Elizabeth goes into seclusion for five months. Her silence is chosen unlike that of her partner.

Before doing this exercise of righteous women in the New Testament, if we were to say to you, who would you have picked to be the one female listed as righteous in the New Testament and furthermore to help you, we narrowed it down to the birth of Jesus, your first choice likely would have been mother Mary. Your second-choice might will have been Anna who recognized the significance of the baby Jesus in the temple. Recall that she prayed regularly at the temple for likely 50-60 years day and night. Those choices would have been reasonable choices, but wrong. Rather it is Elizabeth who is considered righteous.

Keep in mind that God can make anyone righteous and restore by cleansing them. Arguably this is the case for the 4 women listed in Matthew in the linage of Jesus. Two are prostitutes, Tamar and Rahab. Two use methods that some might question such as Bathsheba and Ruth.For some reason that we can only speculate, Mary needs to be connected with them and to use the energy they gained to overcome their past in order to deal with her issues. Somehow, they also need to be connected with Mary to have their stories told and cleansed.

DEBORAH, JUDGE AND PROPHETESS AND MORE

The story of Deborah is contained in the book of judges' chapters 4 and 5. She is the only female judge in the history of Israel. She is also the only judge who was a prophet. In fact, she is one of only five female prophets in the Hebrew Bible. The story begins with the mention that the Israelites had been delivered to their enemies because of evil actions. We read that as a judge, she held regular court. Her judgments were uncontested. In some versions, we are told that she was married, but later interpretation suggest that this was not necessarily the case.

No less than God has determined that it is time to redeem the Israelites. That God sends a message to Deborah to pass on to Barak to lead the Israelites against the enemy. Barak hesitates, noting that he will go only if Deborah goes with him. Deborah affirms, but notes that because of this reluctance, the enemy leader Sisera will be delivered into the hands of a woman. Although we are set up to believe that that woman will be Deborah this is not necessarily the case, though she does go with Barak in the vicinity of the battle.

Then Deborah says to Barak that the Lord will give the enemy leader into his hands. Indeed, this does happen, fulfilling the prophecy of Deborah, although there is a bit of a twist. The enemy leader fleas on foot and goes into a tent. There he is killed by a woman by the name of Jael. Therefore, it would appear that this is the actual woman who gets the credit for killing the enemy. It is indeed a brutal murder where she drives a tent peg with a hammer into his head after showing him some seemingly hospitable gestures. She then shows Barak body of the deceased. That concludes chapter 4.

Chapter 5 is often referred to the song of Deborah. It turns out, though that she actually sang this with the leader that she announced that God had chosen, namely Barak. In that song, she knows that the men of Israel were not willing to fight until Deborah a mother in Israel challenged them. Is this a reference as whether to being married and having children or symbolic figure. Deborah then proceeds to give credit to the volunteers and other fighters in the Israeli army. Meanwhile, Deborah chides men who stayed out of the conflict. There was no taunting Barak because he recognized the benefit of having Deborah there with him.

Then at the close of this song, we have Deborah showing the impact to the enemy King's mother. She envisions her as looking on and waiting for him and wondering when he will return victorious. She even presumes that perhaps the delay is because the enemy is dividing the spoils, including the women. The song concludes with the admonition that all of the enemies of God perish like this. Then we were told that there was peace for 40 years which translates to two generations before the Israelites forgot once again the way of the Lord. Although the irony and ignominy of a mighty warrior falling primarily due to 2 women was not lost in the moment, we wonder why it doesn't get more play time elsewhere.

Hosea And Gomer

We anticipate the very legitimate notion that we will leave out some women of strong influence and character. On the other hand, it is unlikely that if we had left off Gomer from our work that we would have received many complaints. And yet Gomer for all her peculiarities and prostitution, gives us many metaphors that may be derived. She is still one of the most important women in the Original Testament and perhaps of the entire Bible. Gomer is, after all, a prostitute that is used by God to teach both his prophet Hosea as well as the people of Israel about the love of God.

We must keep in mind that although this is a metaphor in which God compares an adulterous wife to the people of Israel and their unfaithfulness, that it is still told as a true story. Perhaps even more surprisingly is that the prophet Hosea is told to go and marry a promiscuous woman or prostitute and furthermore to have children with her. He proceeds to do exactly that and have a son. God chooses the name of Jezreel to signify punishment for a massacre that occurred at that geographic location.

The next thing we see is that Gomer is pregnant and gives birth to a daughter. We are not trying to make anything out of the promiscuity of Gomer, which has already been established. What is not clear initially from the reading is whether or not this daughter belongs to the prophet Hosea. What we are told, though is the name of this daughter translates into "not loved" which represents how God feels towards the people of Israel. Then we see what most of us fear in our everyday lives, which is that the withdrawal of love is equated with the withdrawal of forgiveness.

We are after all told that God will no longer love Israel and thus will not forgive them. Then God appears to emphasize selective love to the people of Judah, who he still plans to save. Shortly, there, after we are told that Gomer had another son and once again we do not know initially who the father is by the reading. The name of this son's name translates into "not my people". God specifically spells out that the people of Israel are not his people and that accordingly this God is not their God.

Even after these strong pronouncements by God, we are still told that the Israelites will be like the sand on the seashore, referencing the metaphors that God gave Abraham. Yet they will still be called the children of the living God for some unknown reason. In chapter 2, God appears to be opening the chapter and speaking to the children of Gomer. Perhaps we find the answer about who the father is not when God says that there will be no love shown to her children because they are the children of adultery.

Then, in the same chapter 2, that God describes the rebuke to Gomer through the children by adultery, we have a turn around by the end of that chapter. Before the end of that chapter, we are told that the people will call God, "my husband" and not my master. We are then told that God will make a covenant which will include the animals on the land and sky and all that moves. God will restore safety and remove violence. Righteousness and justice and love and compassion will triumph. God then takes away the name of "not my people", and replaces it with "you are my people ".

Interestingly, the last that we have of a reference to Gomer appears to be in chapter 3 of the book of Hosea. What we know of her thus far is that she is a prostitute when she marries. After she has one or more children God says to Hosea to go and get his wife again and buy her back and to love her. This is despite the fact that she loves adultery. He gives the analogy that he still loves Israel, even though Israel has turned to other gods and made gifts to those gods. God does point out frankly that Hosea will have to wait a while before Gomer is ready for him just like Israel we have a long wait before they return to their God.

In chapter 4, we start to see the charges of the Lord against the Israelites. This includes lack of faithfulness and lack of acknowledgment of God. In addition, there is cursing and lying and murder and stealing an adultery. There are no boundaries. There is extreme violence. Because of these measures, there is a drying up of the land and the was in the way of all who live in it. Interestingly, we are told in this chapter that God will not punish the daughters or daughters in law when they commit adultery because the men have programmed them for this action.

By chapter 5, the people of Judah are included in those who stumble. By chapter 6, the people of Israel appear ready to repent and change their ways and appeal to God for mercy. However, by chapter 7, there is once again turning away of the people of God from God. God points out that ridicule awaits them. Basically, the rest of the chapters details the consequences of the people of God, turning to idols and all of the destruction that goes with that.

In the closing chapter, we have the apparent words of the prophet Hosea challenging the people of God to return and ask for forgiveness while recognizing that the gods that they have worshiped have not been able to help them. This will allow the anger of God to turn away from them, and cause them to grow stout like the cedars of Lebanon. Then once again they can dwell in the shade and flourish and blossom like the wine. Curiously, we are never told what happens to Gomer after Hosea purchasers her back.

A Surprisingly Powerful Woman

If we were to list in biblical times for sources of potential power and ask you to rank them, would you be able to come up with a satisfactory solution. The choices would be a king , a high priest, God, or a woman. The woman was not by the way, a queen like the influential queen Esther that we have discussed elsewhere. Realistically, our hierarchy would probably start with God and include either the king or the high priest, depending on circumstances.

For the correct answer, we turned to the second book of Kings chapter 22. There we see an eight-year-old boy by the name of Josiah who becomes king. We are told that he followed the ways of the Lord and of his father David, though that was not his direct father, but rather a figure of speech. When Josiah becomes 18 he decides to make some improvements on the temple which, by the way was something that David was never allowed to build because he was a man of war.

Josiah had sent his secretary of state to the high priest of the temple. The high priest uncovers a book of law that was later read in the presence of King Josiah. The words in the book were not comforting because between David and Josiah many generations had deviated greatly from the word of the Lord. Somehow, the high priest had not even known about this deviation until the book was read. This shows how far the traditional authoritarian practice had gone by deviating from some very basic principles.

This was all revealed in the presence of king Josiah, who tore his robes and told the high priest to go inquire of the Lord as to how to mitigate the Lord's anger for disobedience. So what did that high priest do? He went to the prophet Huldah, and she told them straight up. She affirmed the punishment that would have been present, had they not repented. However, she tells the king's contingent that because his heart was responsive, and he humbled himself before the Lord when he heard the words of the Lord that the damages promised would be averted. Arguably, though there is some ambiguity in the promise in which we note that all the disaster would not be brought upon the place, which does not necessarily mean there would be no disaster.

Now it is time for the king to take charge once again, and call all the elders of Judah and Jerusalem together to the temple where they renew the covenant with the Lord. In fact, we have the words that they will renew that covenant with all his heart and all his soul, referring to the king and later to the people in general. Then it was time for house cleaning to do away with the idolatrous priests and all their symbols to the lesser gods, which were perishable. In so doing king Josiah also did away with the practice which allowed young men and women to be sacrificed. Please note that some of the destruction include idolatry connections with the legendary king Solomon.

As much as the Passover had always been a huge Jewish tradition, we are told that there was never an observance of the Passover equal to what Josiah promoted after he eliminated false gods and materialism with the prostitution. This was done when he was a mere 18 years old. King Josiah not only got rid of the major religious connections with idolatry, but also the common household ones from individuals. We read in chapter 23 of Second Kings that there was not a king like him before or after that turned to the Lord with all his heart and with all his soul .

This was all noted early in chapter 23 of Second Kings. Later in the chapter we see the reference of loving God with all his heart, soul, and strength. He appears to gain strength after he has acted. Furthermore, he presages Jesus when he mentions loving God with all your heart, soul, mind, and strength. This would never have come about without the strong convictions of going against the grain that the prophetess Huldah performed. Then too, we must look at the start of Josiah's career at such an early age. Given the wickedness of his father, we might well infer that there is a good reason to mention his mother up front who probably got him his jump start.

JOB

Job And Women

The book of Job has an interesting and arguably, expanding vision of women. To be clear, the start of the book presents us with the typical generational limits of the perspective and rights of women. Because Job is a man of prosperity, it is important for him to have more sons than daughters, according to the dictates and desires of the time. Indeed, this is the case with 7 sons and 3 daughters. To be sure the daughters are invited to the parties that the brothers throw, perhaps because they were a nice attraction for their female friends to be available for their brothers.

The wife of Job does not fair much better. Like the daughters of Job at the start of the book, she remains unnamed. She has a very limited role and one that is often looked at with disdain in sermons and in books. After all, it is she that tells Job to curse God and die. Job answers this very reasonable statement given that he wishes to die with a platitude. In that platitude older versions of the scripture acknowledge that we receive evil from the hand of God. We too, in our modern cultures, are tempted to curse such a God.

The wife of Job is not heard from again after chapter 2. Whatever comparison one wishes to make, such is the case for Satan as well. To be clear, the wife of Job is referenced later on as someone who cannot stand the smell of Job's own breath. She is listed alongside other human possessions of Job, as having no respect for their master. Job, after all, takes great delight and pride, in not only owning things, but having people owe him. Arguably the support system of Job that has traveled far and sat in silence for 7 days while Job bemoaned his woes is symbolic of the typical feminine characteristic of consoling. The fact that Job fails to appreciate this feminine feature may well be representative of his attitude of females in general.

Meanwhile Job feels that he has earned respect that he does not get. He does not perceive his friends who have traveled hundreds of miles to see him and sat in silence while Job cursed the day he was born as sufficiently responding to his needs. He does not appreciate the fact that he has lost his great reputation among the elders. He does not appreciate that things he owns such as his wife, his servants, including men and women do not respect him. He does not appreciate that even boys, whose father cannot hold a candle to him also do not respect him.

Job is after all a good guy as he points out in the wonderful code of his times in chapter 31. Job has respect for women when they are widows as well as orphans, and other people in need. These are people who have some dependence on people like Job which in turn gives Job feathers in his cap. Yet right at the start of this generally wonderful code of the day in chapter 31 we see that Job felt compelled to make a covenant with his eyes to not look lustfully after a young woman. In fact, the term used in many verses is a girl. We might acknowledge that the feeling that he needs to say such a pledge is based on his recognition of a somewhat natural instinct .

There are, however, other potential implications for this phrasing. For example, there is no such pledge against a more mature woman. What we wish to point out here in a more abbreviated fashion, though is the possibility, that even in observance of the code of his day that Job had relations with a young woman, that he later came to realize that although this may have been permitted by the code of his day, it was not necessarily in the best interest of the woman or of society. This may well be what troubles Job about the nighttime with many nightmares and reflections. Please see our work on Job for a more thorough examination of this topic. Arguably the dramatic transformation that occurs at the end of the book of Job is related to his recognition of the need to change the approach for women, as he does, for his own daughters, who now have names and are given an inheritance.

Anachronistic Moralism

Job's righteousness and intervention for his family are held up as a paradigm *by* God to Satan. For now, the stage has been set for a wealthy, pious family member to be exonerated in the presence of angels (1:6 LB). As it turns out, Satan has access to this event as well. Then God asks some questions of Satan that an omniscient God would already have known: "Have you noticed my friend Job? There's no one quite like him-honest and true to his word, totally devoted to God and hating evil" (1:8 MSG). Satan scoffs at this and responds, "Why shouldn't he (turn away from evil) when you pay him so well?" (1:9 LB). Satan then enumerates the many ways God has blessed Job and remarks, "No wonder he 'worships' you" (1:10 LB). The older King James Version projects Satan's retort to God with two questions; this lends itself to be a rhetoric of the two questions to God's earlier two questions. He is jousting, if you will, with God. The Living Bible reduces Satan's question to one. The ERV totally eliminates any questions. All versions, though, portray the joust.

Now the stage has been set for Satan's challenge to God: "But just take away his wealth, and you will see him curse you to your face!" (1:11 LB). The language is biting. Virtually all versions preserve the statement "curse God to his face." Perhaps Job's children have cursed, but they have not done so to God's face. Satan knows this, but he points out that Job will take cursing to the next level. God's reply seems rather casual in the next verse; more or less, it's go ahead, "you may do anything you like with his wealth, but don't harm him physically" (1:13 LB).

Anachronistic Sexism

Job knew evil; he also knew his sons and daughters might know evil as well. Let's be blunt: Job's sons liked to throw parties for his family that included drinking and great merriment (1:5 LB). Furthermore, it appears that Job knew that these parties, which sometimes lasted for days, might have some activities connected with them that could be considered evil. This is evidenced by Job's routine habit of summoning his sons and daughters to him after the nighttime parties and sanctifying them by offering a burnt offering for each of them. Job's perspective was that this was a propitiation for actions connected with them. Job did this early in the morning as though the nighttime activities might have included some spurious acts of a sordid nature they committed.

Being human, we must necessarily speculate on how Job knew to be concerned about activities in the night: "For Job said, 'perhaps my sons have sinned and turned away from God in their hearts'" (1:5 LB). The Living Bible offers the literal interpretation at the bottom explaining having turned away as "have cursed God." Later, I will pursue this cursing thing, the night, and other related topics. Try not to lose sight of the potentially gender-prejudiced nature of this paragraph as it occurs in older versions such as the King James. Some versions attempt to tidy this section into modern inclusive language. While their doing so may be well intended, it misses the contrasts I believe are intended to show through in Job and eventually come out in the end.

These parties were for the sons' honor only (with the sisters invited to share some good times), and the mention of sinning references only his sons in several of the older versions as well as some of the newer ones such as the Living Bible. We can speculate that the daughters did not sin, that the daughters sinned and Job chose not to intercede to God on their behalf, or that the daughters sinned and Job did not know about it. We might speculate further on this last note that even the daughters did not consider some of their actions as sins, but we must be cautious about getting too deep into our dissection too soon. Speculation will not solve our mystery. We need a systematic approach if we are to uncover our proper cause.

Job's Code

After all, we would do well to recall that God indeed calls Job perfect to Satan's face and for all posterity. Satan does not seem to question God's designation of Job as righteous, but he does assert that Job is righteous and perfect solely because of his tremendously blessed status. Yet it becomes obvious as Job unravels more and more in his suffering that the description of perfection really does not pertain to Job. Perhaps some of the conflict experienced by Job, his wife, his friends, everyone in his society is because Job had indeed operated perfectly well according to the moral code of his day. When Job asserts his own "righteousness" to God in chapter 31, he presents a powerful defense of himself as one who strove to avoid lust, deception, covetousness, unfair treatment of others, disregard for the poor and widowed, uncharitable behavior, greediness, revenge, and violence.

He has done a decent job of capturing the moral code, including key portions of the Ten Commandments, codes that one day Jesus would interpret more fully in the Sermon on the Mount, the charge identified in Matthew 25, etc. He has even advanced environmental concerns to make sure that his land does not accuse him of stealing the fruit it bears (31:38 LB). He is even capable of making the key distinction between lust and overt actions several times indicating that he is aware of the difference. And yet he sees a link between thought and action just as Jesus explained in the Sermon on the Mount. Is Job's seemingly obsessive desire to protest his innocence regarding lust a hint at what may have beep the sin (with one more nod to Shakespeare: "The lady dost protest too much methinks" Hamlet act 3, stene 2])? Lene 21)?

It would appear strange if that were so because Job clearly states what judgment falls on those who "look with lust upon a girl" (31:1 *LB*). He states unequivocally, "I know full well that Almighty God above sends calamity on those who do. He sees everything I do, and every step I take" (31:2-3 LB).

Job is every man, woman, boy, and girl in that it is a universal trait of humans to believe themselves morally superior to others. Job describes how he has done his best to live a good life. He has made a covenant, a commitment to being a good person. If he isn't perfect, at least in his own mind, he is closer to it than are many people. And that should count for something.

ADULTERY 1

Why does Job have nightmares anyway? For that matter, why do any of us have nightmares? Most psychologists and dream analysts say we have nightmares over unresolved issues. Some of these psychologists will add that there are no such things as frightening dreams, that there are only frightened dreamers. Job knows full well that nighttime may be a time for sexual activity. He refers earlier to having been conceived in the night. He goes on to reference some of his own issues in his younger days and how God must be holding those against him now. "You write bitter things against me and bring up all the follies of my youth" (13:26 LB). The King James Version uses the word iniquities rather than follies as do several others. It is as though something of his youth wasn't quite right, but he isn't willing to use the word *sin* here. Several versions, including the King James, point out that Job inherited these iniquities of youth as though they were part of his inescapable DNA. Job does not equate these follies with adultery.

Adultery, after all, would carry a harsher penalty than those youthful follies. We have already referenced Job's allusion to adultery as a situation with another man's wife when the description of the moral code is given from chapter 31. This code connects adultery only with another man's wife and does not specifically preclude other activities, namely, a man's sexual relationship with an unmarried woman who just might happen to be desirous. "The desires of my heart turn night into day," notes Job (17:11–12 NIV).

Job 31 appears to have much to offer for a moral compass even if it is the last long speech of defense for a self-righteous individual. We can appreciate the opening verse of avoiding lust even if we're not familiar with Jesus's admonition in the New Testament, but what happens if we examine it from another perspective that cannot readily be refuted?

ADULTERY 2

The fact that Job made a covenant against lust toward a young woman means that he certainly knew about lust. In fact, this passage does not rule out Job having lust at an earlier age and making the pledge later. Indeed, *if* we consider that both the reference to adultery later and lust for a younger woman coupled with action could be ruinous, we may shed some different light. But to whom exactly would this be ruinous? It would certainly affect *Job* and people of means like him. It would affect his precious reputation. Job senses a strong connection between lust and action- perhaps even an action that he had committed before and that he can ill afford in his blessed state of wealth. Despite his wealth, he can ill afford to even consider lust. But what about reconsidering the consequences about the other party?

Job's original perception of his sin is that he did not harm God or his understanding of God. One wonders if that is so given the way the story unfolds.

Perhaps that is Job's understating of the application of the moral code at the initiation of his ordeal.

Perhaps through introspection, suffering, mockery, nightmares, and other challenges, Job arrives at a new understanding of the code.

Perhaps this understanding leads Job to realize that some people have been harmed even unintentionally by the old code.

ADULTERY 3

Perhaps this is the dawning of Job's awareness of his limited understanding of the covenant he has made.

Elihu has cut deeply. He has opened old wounds that Job did not realize he had. There may even be some scarring that miraculously Job has not seen. Elihu has exposed the reality that moral certainty is not in the capacity of Job or any other human being. Job is lying naked on the exam table; his reputation cannot help him there.

As deep as Elihu's cut is, Job needs someone like Elihu, the messenger, the intercessor, to help him realize the full extent of his new covenant. After all, Job cannot figure out all the suffering, mockery, nightmares, etc., by himself. As a warm-up for the nighttime challenges, Elihu tells Job, "No darkness is thick enough to hide evil from his eyes, so there is no need to wait for some great crime before a man is called before God in judgement" (34:22-23 LB).

Are you listening, Job? God has already seen your nighttime activities, and by the way those activities don't necessarily have to have been considered that bad to still have major significance. Elihu says, "Do not desire the nighttime, with its opportunities for crime. Turn back from evil, for it was to prevent you from getting into a life of evil that God sent you this suffering" (36:20–21 LB). There you have it, Job. You asked for your day in court to learn why you are suffering - something you did in the night that you desired strongly and really did not think was all that bad is actually evil. That is why you have all this suffering. Jog wanted his day in court, but it is the night that judged him.

Job's Conclusion 1

Ultimately, the book of Job *is* about sacrifice. Whether or not you agree with any of my other speculations, you cannot escape the conclusion that the book of Job is pervasive in its theme of sacrifice. The book is framed with sacrifice; it appears in the first and the concluding chapter. While those sacrifices are rather obvious, the rest of the book is infused with numerous allusions to sacrifice.

The first chapter finds Job making a blood sacrifice for his children. We have already noted that in several references, such sacrifice was for his sons only, not his daughters. Other versions are more inclusive and note that the sacrifice was for them all. Either way, it was not enough if the goal was to keep them alive through atonement justice; they die later in the same chapter.

What is more, Job has no more traditional animals to sacrifice even if he felt like it. Those animal deaths have preceded the deaths of his sons and daughters as if to set the stage and dramatize their deaths. We certainly want to avoid the all too human thinking that perhaps Job didn't have the right attitude and that resulted in the rejection of his sacrifice in a sense. We also enter with caution the paradoxical waters that suggest Job had his own sin to atone for. After all, after this tragic ordeal, God labels Job as perfect. While this sense of perfection has been analyzed by scholars and not felt to have the same meaning as one who never sinned, we are still left to feel that whatever sacrifices Job has made, they were not enough.

Job's Conclusion 2

Job will spend the next forty chapters sacrificing what little he has left. He has sacrificed his possessions, next his family, next his health. Sacrificing his pride, though, seems to be as hard as any sacrifice he will make until he realizes he must sacrifice his very ideas about God and justice.

Just when we think Job has been humbled enough by God, Elihu, his three friends, and life's events, Job must face one final sacrifice in front of his friends. They will bring animals out of their abundance and sacrifice them in front of Job. Job is then obliged to pray for them so they may be forgiven. This is the double slap in the face. Job has no more animals and could use a few of these prime animals about to be sacrificed. He could also use a break from his friends whose well-intended jabs have stung worse than his physical afflictions. Job has to sacrifice his pride and his understanding of God when it becomes clear that the friends' sacrifice achieved the goal while his own in chapter 1 hadn't achieved his. It is almost as though Job is sacrificing his own idea of sacrifice.

After this act of propitiation, Job's fortunes begin to return. In fact, his restoration of good fortune does not happen until he prays for those he perceived as inadequate support; indeed, it begins precisely at that point. "Then, when Job prayed *for* his friends, the Lord restored his wealth and happiness!

JOB'S CONCLUSION 3

The humbled, repentant, and forgiven Job has the opportunity for instant restoration with others as well. "Then all *of* his brothers, sisters and former friends arrived and feasted with him at his home, consoling him for all his sorrows and comforting him because of the trials the Lord had brought upon him" (42:11 LB). Further blessings are bestowed on Job including the return of his wealth and children but only after Job accepts the condolences of his friends and family. Job has much to show for having endured the whirlwind of suffering and God's challenges. Yes, God has brought these trials upon Job (42:11 any version), but Job has also imagined and experienced his grievances (36:17 LB).

Once this awareness dawns upon the various parties, Job will seek to make amends by the only true change he performs, which comes after the personal chastising by Elihu and God and the offerings of propitiation for his three friends and finally after accepting consolation from those friends and family. Job has yet to receive his final blessing and perhaps make amends for the sin. Job is given seven more sons and three more daughters. In contrast to chapter 1, the daughters are given names, unlike the seven sons, and they are acknowledged for their beauty (42:13-15 any version).

Job's Conclusion 4

Better yet, and far ahead *of* the times, these daughters are included in his will. That way, they do not need to be fearful of being taken advantage of because of their "desirous nature" and losing their reputation and wealth (as still happens in much of the world today). In particular, they do not need to fear being taken advantage of by an older wealthy male who has a good daytime reputation.

A case can be made that Job's sin, "the" sin, was taking advantage of a young woman; neither he nor society considered this an indiscretion at the time. Just as Job contributed to the staining of a young woman's reputation, so too is his reputation stained. When the whirlwind shakes Job's sensory awareness, he is given an opportunity to move beyond his moral certainty that Satan never accomplished from his unwavering position. A new covenant has been forged based on a new understanding, and this supersedes yet complements the code of God as understood by Job and is manifest in social change. It's inspiring when people come to their senses and recognize that their limited understanding and self-preoccupation manifested in their biases and prejudices are stopping them from performing acts that would lead to a more inclusive society.

Our postmortem examination has given us new insights into the struggles of Job and the meaning of new life. Moral certainty died with Satan obviously but less obviously when the God of Job's earlier awareness died. An autopsy is not an aimless procedure performed out of curiosity; rather, it is performed for those living to receive insight into their own lives. It may inspire us to avoid certain toxicities including thoughts as well as actions. It may inspire us to include other measures that improve our quality of life.

DAVID AND SOLOMON

THE MOST POWERFUL WOMEN IN DAVID'S LIFE

We are accustomed to David being attracted to beautiful women. This is no surprise. What may come as more of a surprise is that female power may be a larger attraction for David when it comes to women. For example, we are never told how attractive his first wife, Michal, the daughter of a king was. However, she represented power. Indeed, her connections helped to save David's life on at least one occasion. However, once she has served his purpose, he will have nothing to do with her. However, he will not let anyone else have her after she has been taken away and become the partner of another. Rather he will go to some length to get her back, only to ignore her again.

No one is going to question the beauty of Bathsheba. However, there is a fair chance that equally attractive to David was her wit and cunning ability. We have noted elsewhere that given a city the size of Jerusalem at the time and the importance of Uriah, that David and Bathsheba already knew each other. They likely calculated their affair, just as David ultimately calculated the cold death of his loyal general Uriah. In fact, an argument can be made that beauty alone was not enough to motivate David if power was not there with the woman.

Consider the case of Abishag. We are told that she was the most beautiful woman in the land. Keep in mind that Bathsheba was still alive at this time. Abishag comes into David's life at the end of his life. This is all well documented in First Kings in the first book of the first chapter. David has lost his Mojo. His advisers are well aware of this as he has no energy and is cold all of the time. Naturally these advisors seek out what would generally motivate king David. They find the most beautiful woman in all the land to lie by David and motivate him. Their intention appears quite clear. There is only one problem with the plan.

David is not up to the task. David appears unable to consummate the relationship with the most beautiful woman in the world. We may argue it is because it is the end of his life and his testosterone is deficient. We do find that by the way. immediately in the next verse that this appears to be a signal to his usurpers of the throne anyway to move on the king. We must keep in mind the alternate explanation in that David did not find sufficient motivation for consummation because at that time Abishag did not have power.

What happens next has not been matched by today's sordid novels. Adonijah senses the opportunity to seize the throne. Queen Bathsheba realizes that she must aet quickly and gets key leaders, both religious and military on her side. They thwart the uprising. This potential usurping son of David known as Adonijah seeks mercy. Interestingly, after he is granted this, he asked for the queen to go to his brother Solomon and ask if it would not be too much to have Abishag for himself.

It is the recognition by king Solomon, that this is not merely lustful or hormonal opportunity to be with the most beautiful woman in the land. Rather, it is a signal to the community at large that Adonijah son of David could do what David himself could not do. Quite likely queen Bathsheba knew that this would be the outcome of the request and let if play out in order that Adonijah would be killed and not hang around unlike the deceased son Absalom, who rose up in revolt against his father king David. Thus, whether directly or indirectly, Abishag contributes to the death of one king and another pretender to the throne. Her power, though, was more passive and came only after her connection with David and was coincidental at that.

DAVID'S MOTIVATION

In one of our earlier essays, we borrowed from our book on David And Michaelangelo as to the motivation of David. For example, what was it that actually motivated David to fight Goliath? Commonly in sermons, David is portrayed as the humble shepherd boy who is attending to his older brothers in the army when the giant named Goliath from the Philippines taunts the Israelites. Please keep in mind the reality that David had already proved himself in battle as we read about in earlier chapters in the Bible.

When David hears of the taunts of the giants, he asked what is in it for himself if he takes on the giant and wins. There will be land, money and tax breaks and a woman. David may have been a poor shepherd boy, but his needs were already met in terms of land and money. He was a man driven by his hormones and accordingly it would appear that he fought Goliath as much for a woman as anything. When the king fails to deliver on his end of the bargain after the victory, David performs another heroic task to win another one of the king's other daughters.

All of his life women will represent a strong drive for David. It is only at the end of his life when he loses that drive that there is a signal to David's competition that his end is near. We will have more to say on that elsewhere. David is motivated by beauty and power and in particular when the two are matched up with women. Such is the case with his first wife. It also appears to be the case with his wife, Abigail, as well as ultimately with Bathsheba. As we have noted in our book, David and Michelangelo, the Bathsheba affair appears to have been calculated on both sides.

Whereas the outcome of this story in the first union of David and Bathsheba is the death of that procreation, we may find it interesting of how David consoles his grieving partner. If you guessed that it was to have sex with her, then you are correct. This is all detailed in the story. Keep in mind that as strong as attraction of beauty was for David with Bathsheba, that other strong attractions for Bathsheba included that her husband was a successful warrior and likely that David already knew about her ability to be shrewd.

Bathsheba's husband, Uriah was not only a very successful warrior, but also served as a role model for David and even a Christlike symbol as we have detailed in our book David and Michaelangelo. Our purpose here though is to point out that whereas there are some powerful individuals whom you do not wish to be in debt to, the opposite is the case here. You do not want David to be indebted to you.

Debt as a tool is a powerful motivation for David to turn his back on you or outright kill you.

We have already mentioned how he turned his back on Michal who saved his life. David will also put to death his key General Joab, who killed the insurrectionist son of David, Absolom. David will have several people put to death involving their roles in the deaths of David's enemy kings. Such is the case after Saul's death when his son sits on the throne. Even more incredulously is that he will have a messenger put to death merely because he is bringing the new that David's enemy King Saul has been put to death.

David's Anger Over Family Incest And Rape

We are told that David was upset about the event of the rape of his daughter Tamar. There is some ambiguity about what David was upset about. Word of the rape of Tamar by her half- brother filtered up to King David. Although he was enraged, he did not discipline him. Amnon's brother Absalom quit talking to him. it might seem obvious that David was upset about the rape, but keep in mind that Tamar herself felt the worst consequence of the whole event was the rejection she received by the violator half-brother Amnon because she desired a marriage that David would not support.

Then too, David could be upset because he was pulled into the plot of the seduction of Tamar. In such a case as this, David might be upset more with Amnon than the rape itself because he was pulled into the case. David might have been too busy to deal with a trifling matter of the rape of one of his daughters by one of his sons. David may have been upset with the event because it called attention to his own weakness in many ways. This includes his own misplaced hormonal drives as well as his poor parenting skills.

Conceivably David was upset with himself because he did not see coming what should have been obvious to a man with David's experience and hormones. After all, Amnon essentially describes that he wishes to watch his half-sister Tamar prepare him a special meal. Another possibility is that David is upset, not so much about the rape, but the fact that Amnon refused to ask Tamar to marry him. Another consideration is that David is upset because Amnon hates Tamar after the event. Another possibility here is that David is actually upset with Absolom because he does nothing to vindicate the rape. In somewhat of an ironic fashion, David could be upset with Absolom because Absolom does not say anything to Amnon after that whether good or bad. Finally, David might be upset because of the Bathsheba affair, which was just getting resolved in the previous chapter.

After Absalom goes into exile for the whole event, one of David's generals will send a widow from Tekoa with a contrived story that will tug on David's sense of justice. The pretentious widow offers some platitudes that are almost too irresistible for David. She appeals further to David's ego with flattery. While David appears to catch on to the deception, he does relent and allow Absalom to come home. In a strange twist of events that key general Joab ultimately kill Absalom when the latter becomes an insurrectionist. As we note in our book on David and Michelangelo, in this entire story, there does not seem to be genuine repentance or genuine forgiveness.

Ultimately, David cannot be indebted to anyone. This is why he had to have Joab killed at the end of his life, even though Joab had saved David's life from the insurrectionist son. Indeed, it is conceivable that David actually greatly admired Absolom and his willingness to deliver justice where David had failed. Somehow, he needed to teach him how to be a better person and a better family man and better deliverer of justice. In many ways Absolom is very much like David's best friend Jonathan, who is willing to sacrifice himself for the cause. Keep in mind that, although we are told that David never loved anyone, man, or woman more than he loved Jonathan, that David is missing in a key battle and which arguably he could have made a difference for Jonathan's life. Jonathan who was closer than a brother dies with the mighty warrior David hiding in fear.

WOMEN OF DAVID

Many of David's wives share some features of having connection with power and men of power. As we noted some of these women have been connected with powerful individuals and had been wives to other men such as Uriah and Nabal. At least two of his wives have been daughters of kings, including Michal. David seems to be attracted to this level of power, intelligence, and shrewdness, etc. He is not troubled if the women have belonged to someone else first. However, once there is evidence that women of David have been used by other men after having been in David's possession, he appears to have very little to do with them. Such is clearly the case of 10 of his wives/concubines whom he left behind when he fled Jerusalem, only to have them despoiled by Absalom. Subsequent to that David had no relations with them. This also appears to be the case of Michal who is given away by king Saul to another man, even after she had married David only to be ultimately returned. However, following that return there is no indication that he had relations with her again.

What about the women in David's own family? Given that we have only a handful of stories we have no choice, but to take those as illustrative of the challenges David posed. In the story of Amnon, David takes his non-interventional strategy to the maximum. That ultimate challenge comes when Amnon rapes his half-sister Tamar. Absolom is quite upset about this. On one hand, he does not want to disturb the king too much on this matter, or the divine right of Kings and their heirs to take certain liberties. On the other hand, we are told that David did not want to say anything in this case, in order to avoid upsetting Amnon. Indeed, David is paralyzed to intervene.

Whatever happened to David's first wife Michal? First, we return to the story in which David fights Goliath. Please keep in mind that David was already an established hero before this as the Bible clarity demonstrates. We ask ourselves why did David fight Goliath.? For those of faith it is simply that God was using David for victory over the enemy Philistines. However, David would not fight Goliath until it was clarified what was in it for him. That answer was that there was some land, some money or riches and the king's daughter. We argue that the first two did not mean much to a young man who had all of his needs on the land that he worked already bech met and would not know what to do with if he had more anyway. However, he was a hormonal, young man and knew what he wanted with a woman. Especially the King's daughter.

Let's forget temporarily that David did not get what he was pledged at that moment with that particular daughter of the king that was promised. Rather, he has to go through another ordeal to prove himself. Later that daughter Michal will save his life when David is fleeing from here father the King. In addition, David will later to to some lengths to have her retrieved after she has been stolen and become another person's partner. What is the price that she will pay for all of this? Rather, he last to go through another order to prove himself. Later that daughter, Michal, will save his life when David is fleeing from her father the king. In addition, David will later go to some lengths to have her retrieved after she had been stolen and become another person's partner. What is the price that she will pay for all of this?

She will be ignored by David upon her return. Furthermore, as she remained childless, much to David dismay and yet own responsibility, she adapts children from someone in the family. David will ultimately have those children brutally murdered.

All of this was predicted in advance by Samuel before Israel ever had a king in that he noted kings would take various liberties, with this prediction and David's genetics and the hormones of young man, how could Amnon think any differently. He asks his half-sister Tamar a sexist request to make him dinner when he feigns a sickness. David is, after all, the king of imagination and deceit and should have seen this coming. After all, would we not expect a king who pretends to be crazy to think that one of his sons might pretend to be sick in order to have a little intimacy with incest?

THE WOMAN FROM TEKOA

We might as well call this essay three women and king David. We begin the story starting in the sixth chapter of second Samuel. David has completed a successful campaign against his enemies and wished to celebrate by bringing the ark of God to a new location. In fact, the preferred destination was Jerusalem also known as the city of David. The first attempt led to the death of an individual who merely tried to steady the ark of God when it moved. Apparently God did not feel the need to be steadied and struck the individual dead on the spot.

This act caused David to be angry with God, but also to fear God. After the ark rested a while at a place that was blessed because of the presence of the ark, David decided again that it was his prerogative to move the ark of God. The new journey lasted six steps Before David determined that it was time to celebrate. David danced before the people in what some versions have determined may have been a lewd fashion and his wife Michal called him out on this. David takes out his vengeance on her for the rest of her life as we have discussed in a separate section in our book David and Michelangelo.

Then David seems to enjoy peace to the extent that God's number one prophet Nathan visits David and makes a promise to David through God about their future relationship as well as where God may be worshiped. This pledge will be delivered through the offspring of David. David then proceeds to have more victories over his enemies. He determines it is time to pay back a promise that he made to his best friend Jonathan, who is killed in a battle that the mighty warrior David did not bother to show up for. David brings the only remaining offspring of the house of king Saul and Jonathan, who is a crippled individual who will live in the palace and enjoy the food directly from the king's table.

David is on a roll and must feel very blessed. Accordingly, he goes to war and has some more victories. However, it would appear that David does not relish moments of peace. After all of these victories and blessings, we note in chapter 11 that in the spring of the year when Kings go off to war, that David determined it was that time again. However, David has become a stay-at-home king and sent out his number one general Joab to do the duties. During this time he has his encounter with Bathsheba, which we have detailed elsewhere in our book mentioned.

When the loyal general Uriah, husband of Bathsheba, does not go along with the plot that David has orchestrated, David has his top general, Joab, place Uriah in a strategic place of the battle, such that he will be killed. Following this the same prophet Nathan, who has listed David a few chapters earlier will approach David and give a parable about the poor man whose sheep was sacrificed for the rich man. Nathan, then notes that David will be subjected to have the metaphorical sword in his house, and the house of his offspring forever. Although David is forgiven, the baby conception of that relationship with Bathsheba becomes ill and dies. In classic David fashion he consoles the mother Bathsheba by having sex with her and producing Solomon.

We next see the unfolding of the prophecy regarding the sword, in the house of David start to be fulfilled beginning in chapter 13. In that chapter, we have the incestuous relationship with one of David's sons Amnon with his half-sister Tamar. When David does nothing about this encounter, another son Absolom, who happens to be the brother of Tamar, kills Amnon. The social media of the day delivers a fake message to King David that all of the kings sons have been killed and repeats the message that not one is left.

The fact checkers of the day correct the report and note that only Amnon has been killed. However, Absolom has now fled. He has been gone for three years when David's top general Joab recognizes that king David wishes to be united with Absolom. Joab sends a messenger to the nearby village of Tekoa for a wise woman to be brought to him. Together they devise a plot which involves another parable not unlike that which the prophet Nathan did a few chapters earlier. She was told to act like a woman who is grieving for her lost child who had been murdered by the brother. The widow acts concerned because the law requires that the murderous son be put to death as well. However, this son is her only legacy and source of income and support.

David, then intervenes and said that such a death will not occur on his watch. The wise woman then calls out David much like the prophet Nathan had called him out earlier over his sin. David senses that his general Joab has been behind all of this and confronts the so-called widow about this. Interestingly, when she acknowledges the connection, king David turns to the general Joab and says, very well and he instructs him to bring back the exiled son Absolom. However, two years go by and King David has refused to see Absalom.

Finally, after much effort, Absalom is united with his father King David. He then precedes to take advantage of the situation and build up a group of followers over the next four years. Then the son of deception who has learned from the master of deception, decides that it is timed to strike against his father King David. Perhaps because King David has now been out of the action of fighting for sometime he determines that it is in a survival interest to flee the city.

So it would appear that the mighty king David has become soft and quite possibly because he had not been fighting , but also because he had hardened his heart. This process would appear to begin when he hardens his heart against his wife Michal, who has saved his life and then was psychologically exiled because of trying to have him express decency in front of people. Perhaps then, David realized that his life was truly on public display when he tried to do the private act with Bathsheba. The problem is was that such was never really a private act, but was known by many people and arguably orchestrated between king David and Bathsheba. Finally, the widow of Tekoa comes and tries to soften the heart of David. While she does appear to accomplish some of that, it would appear that David hardened his heart shortly there after.

During this stretch, we have David abandoning his wife who has saved his life. Then he abandons his morals and has his not so private affair. He next abandons his children in their hour of need. He then abandons attempts at reconciliation with his son. Then, because all of these measures speak of fear, he acts on that fear and abandons the kingdom that God has given him and promises him. The combination of fear has led to a hardened approach by king David. If he could not appeal to his own feminine side, he might have done well to listen to the feminine voices in his life who are trying to give him direction as opposed to merely an erection.

David And The Make Believe Woman

We have seen a picture painted of David in this treatise, as well as in our book David and Michelangelo, the Heart and Stone in which David uses women to his own ends. David certainly seems well-versed at using women of power as well as wealth and influence. We must allow that when David could not perform sexually at the end of his life for the most beautiful woman around that such was not merely a reflection of his waning testosterone at the end of his life, but also a reflection that perhaps the problem was that the woman had a very meager background and was not a woman of power that David typically favored.

However, in this essay, we will make our case that David once used a woman for a dastardly deed, who did not even exist. To unravel the details of this story, you must turn to second Samuel chapter 11. There we are told the story of David and Bathsheba . You must appreciate the economy of the Scriptures that in four verses begin with David who cannot sleep and apparently does not know who Bathsheba was. He then sends for her to come to the palace where he sleeps with her and gets her pregnant. That's the story. Four verses.

The problem is that Bathsheba is the wife of someone else, namely Uriah, who is one of David's leading generals. He is also incredibly loyal. David calls Uriah from the front lines and attempts to bring him home in order that he may sleep with his wife Bathsheba, and then be free from the paternity claim. King David tries to get him to do the deed by giving Uriah gifts. This does not work. He does get Uriah drunk, but even in his drunken state Uriah refuses to sleep with his wife while there is a major war going on.

When this plot by King David fails, David feels that his only choice is to put in writing to his top general Joab that Uriah is to be stuck on the front line where the fighting is fierce. Then at the height of the battle, the general Joab is to command soldiers to do something that they would not do under the most extreme of circumstances. They are to pull away from Uriah in order that he will be struck down and killed. Some other innocent bystander soldiers are part of the package of death as collateral damage.

What was the symbolism of the death of Uriah? Consider the following: 1) He was a totally innocent man. 2) A powerful king sought his death. 3) He resisted temptation, even in challenging circumstances. 4) He was spied upon within his own circle. 5) He was betrayed and abandoned by those closest to him. 6) He was vilified. 7) He was a servant who suffered. 8) He died an ignominious death. As you can see the loyal warrior, Uriah is a symbolic presage of the Christ. Yet David will employ some identity theft to assume these traits as his own.

So where does the nonexistent woman come into the story? David allows his key general Joab to circulate a story that makes it appear as though the mighty warrior Uriah may have been killed by a woman. Furthermore, it was the experienced warrior Uriah who should have known that getting close too close to the enemy wall, could indeed lead to death. We can debate that. However, the mighty King David seems quite content to not only take Uriah's wife before his death, but also to make sure that this Christ like figure Uriah is discredited long after his death by a woman who did not even exist. God will have the last say, however. In giving the lineage of Jesus in the New Testament, we see that Bathsheba is listed as the wife of Uriah and not of David.

DAVID AND THE PIVOTAL WOMAN

I will frequently listen to the Beatles station on Sirius satellite in order to hear the background stories that go beyond the music. Many of the commentators on the channel have had firsthand exposure to the band and its members. They have an intimate familiarity with both the music and its evolution and the setting that produced it. During an interview of one such individual, they asked him to name which song separated best the early period of the Beatles and the later period of the Beatles. The person asking that question had a specific answer in mind which the individual himself proceeded to name the exact song.

As impressive as this was, I would maintain that the widow woman of Tekoa represents the great intersection of David and the women in his life. Keep in mind her basic background in that she has already a woman who has lost her husband. She has had a son who was murdered. That son was murdered by the other son and she stands therefore to lose this son as well and everything that such a son represents in that time frame. We have already detailed how this widow represents women from the proceeding chapters before encounter with David. She will, however, continue to represent, David and his relationship to women for the rest of his life.

First, we see that she stands in for his wife Michal, who saved his life, only to be ignored and shunned for the rest of life after she points out one of the public faults of David. Yet David cannot stand the situation when she is taken from him and possessed by another man. Therefore, he will fight to get her back only to ignore her again following that return of his property. The final chapter for Michal comes when she adopts children given that David will have no relationship with her only to ultimately have those same children brutally murdered by David.

Of course, the widow represents queen Bathsheba at some level. She is after all a widowed woman who has lost her husband, quite possibly in defense of king David and his many wars while David is elsewhere much like the time he was missing in action when his best friend Jonathan was killed. This would make such a husband, not unlike Uriah, who was set up to be murdered by King David in order to, acquire Bathsheba for his harem. She is furthermore like queen Bathsheba who has lost one child and fears losing a second.

As to Tamar, the daughter of David, who was raped by one of David 's sons, the woman represents someone who has been violated and has no means to support herself. Tamar might have been able to secure the best of a bad relationship had David forced the half brother to marry Tamar, just like David could make the best of a bad situation for the widow by saving the one son who had murdered the brother and make the best out of that bad situation. Strange as it may seem, after the rape, Tamar requested of her rapist half-brother Amnon to go to king David and ask for permission for the relationship which she surmised David would surely grant.

As the intersection of women and David's life, the widow of Tekoa will go on to represent women who are ignored or mistreated by David following this event. We would not be surprised that David's fixation with having a male heir would ultimately lead to the return of Absalom, who would then go on to take over the kingdom and proceed to violate women who belonged to David. And why not? What did David do when his own daughter was violated? Nothing. Absolutely nothing. For the concubines involved David will ignore them for the rest of their lives meaning that they probably lost their status and economic support.

Yes, the wise widow of Tekoa gets the attention of David briefly. She is one of the few women in his life who will singe his conscience. However, David and Joab are content to have Absalom nearby where they can keep an eye on him without reconciling which would have been the true intention of the widow even though it was not necessarily that of Joab or David. Absalom will subsequently resort to violence to see his father King David which leads to his ultimate death and a strange weeping by David, given that the son would have certainly killed David. All of this happened because David did not listen to the wise feminine voice of the widow from Tekoa who sought justice through reconciliation. As much of a representation as David might be for us today, we would do well to complete his unfulfilled mission of reconciliation as promoted by the wise widow.

SOLOMON: WISDOM, PROSTITUTES, AND UNWED MOTHERS – PART 1

After Solomon is established as the rightful king, with the help of the right clergy, and his mother, queen Bathsheba, we get the final days of the life of David. They are filled with a horrific vengeance on people from events far earlier in his life. Such is the case of one of his former generals, who was popular himself, crushed an uprising against one of the other sons. Also included is the poor man who taunted David, and was let go at the moment, only to be killed by the instructions of David given at the end of the life of David. We do not see in these vengeful statements and commands by the dying King David, to seek wisdom for his son who is to be king Solomon. No, rather David, dies with vengeance as his motive.

There is no death scene with father to son advice about what to do or to avoid making some of the mistakes that David did. What we have in the early kingship of Solomon is the following. He will have one of David's key generals put to death. This was a dying request from his father David. He will have someone who insulted David years earlier put to death. He will have the brother who lead the charge to take over the kingship from David put to death not because of that fact, but rather, for the fact that he wish to consummate the relationship with the beautiful woman that king David was unable to do. Now we can move on to the next chapter. King Solomon will take the daughter of an Egyptian pharaoh somewhat in turn about from the story we find from the experience of Abraham and Isaac at an earlier time in Genesis.

It is only at this time in chapter 3 of first Kings that it is finally time for King Solomon to ask for wisdom. Apparently, he did not need any wisdom to put key people to death who were associated with his father, including family. He already had an example in that in his father, and he could follow that. Apparently, he did not need wisdom to marry the daughter of a king. He already had plenty of examples again from his father, David who enjoyed beautiful women of high status, married or otherwise. No, we maintain that Solomon asked for wisdom because he saw that David really did not have it and that ending your life with vengeance was not a particularly wise thing to do as it showed a tremendous lack of forgiveness with all its toxic consequences. These are the circumstances of the wisdom seeking Solomon as the prelude to that acquisition. What is his first application of that wisdom? It's all right there in the third chapter of first Kings. King Solomon will settle a dispute between two prostitutes. He will not judge them for their prostitution, but rather will recognize one of the prostitute's legitimate rights to her baby, however that baby was conceived. Now, perhaps we have wisdom.

SOLOMON: WISDOM, PROSTITUTES, AND UNWED MOTHERS – PART 2

We have already reviewed at link of the timing of the acquisition of Solomons wisdom. It would appear that Solomon felt the need for wisdom, after carrying out the vengeance acts on behalf of his father king David, who was full of vitriolic retribution for people who had been associated with him. Solomon proceeds to carry out those violent acts of killing. Then he marries the daughter of a foreign king. Now, perhaps he can have sweet dreams. Indeed, he has a dream in which God comes to him in that dream, and asks Solomon what he would desire. Solomon may not yet be wise but he is also no dummy.

A dream, of course, is a reflection of the subconscious. Perhaps before he went to bed the night before his dream, Solomon was legitimately concerned about having nightmares given the acts of vengeance that he had performed just because his father King David could not come to terms with some measures himself at the end of his life. Nonetheless, Solomon has a dream in which he senses God coming to him and asking Solomon what it was that he desired most. We maintain the Solomon saw that he needed more wisdom than his spiteful father king David, in order to govern people. Perhaps, after having his own brother put to death, King Solomon thought that there might be a better way. Perhaps he realized that marrying a rich beautiful woman like his father had done with the queen Bathsheba, his mother, was not enough for him even though Solomon had already had that marriage already before his wisdom.

So in his dream Solomon is indeed granted the wisdom and discernment that he was seeking. He gets a bonus of riches and a long life because of his request. Of course, wisdom is not useful unless it is put to the test. That is what the rest of chapter 3 in First Kings is about. What better test of wisdom could we have than being approached by two unwed mothers about a property dispute? Did we mention that they were prostitutes? Did we mention that the property dispute was about a baby?

The story is all right there in chapter 3 of first Kings. Both of these unwed mothers were living together perhaps out of convenience for the prostitution work. Both of them became pregnant around the same time. Might even have been the same man which would promote more easily the potential for the bizarre forthcoming baby swap. After a few days, one of the mother's baby died after she slept on it. Apparently, they did not have all the information about SIDS that was available to watch these days. That mother takes the infant from the other mother in that fateful night, and puts the dead baby under the other mother's side. The following morning, the change is discovered. The woman whose baby is still alive understandably very much wishes to have her baby back and appeals to King Solomon.

Let's look at his wisdom and judgment in this case. First of all, he does not judge the women because of their profession of prostitution. Secondly, he does not judge them for being unwed mothers. He does not judge the mother who killed her baby, figuring that this could be a legitimate action on her part without knowing that much about SIDS. No, rather his first major decision after his acquisition of wisdom is to have the baby killed. Better yet he will do it himself with a sword, and makes that command. Now at this point, both of the women probably know that Solomon has just recently killed people for grievances years ago, and killed, famous and popular generals, and killed his own brother. They have to believe he is serious about this. So do we.

We cannot make simple assumptions that Solomon knew what the outcome would be with one woman that the other rightful mother could have the baby. That is only obvious to us, in hindsight. When we reflect on the first major decision after his acquisition of wisdom, and the only decision in that first chapter of his wisdom, we perhaps can learn some valuable lessons. Perhaps it is wise for us not to judge people for their profession. Perhaps it is wise for us not to judge those who are unwed mothers. Perhaps some leniency is best when even major accidents happen. Perhaps we, too, should pray for wisdom, when we have been asked to do acts of violence on the behalf of others. Perhaps we, too, should pray for wisdom, when we have performed such acts of violence.

NEW TESTAMENT PART 1

BORN OF A WOMAN – PART 1

For the purpose of this essay, the reader would do well to read the excellent work by Bishop John Shelby Spong: Born Of A Woman. There the bishop will explore the significance of the myth of the Virgin birth. In addition, he will demonstrate historically how this myth arose, and how it was both perpetuated and perpetrated in the later early church. This myth was not necessarily a part of the first generation of Christians, including Paul, who wrote his works, approximately one generation, after the death of Jesus, well before any gospel was written. Mr. Spong will note that cultures, which promoted the concept of virginity tended to have a less respect historically for females. At the times the gospels were written there would only be a scandal in the absence of virginity only if the pre-marital sexual acts did not involve her intended partner.

    The original presentation of Jesus, as a baby in the temple, involves the purification right of a natural birth. Mr. Spong relies heavily on the concept of the gospel of Luke being a pageant that was reworked over time to include additional elements that fit the Jewish calendar. This included The insertion of measures like the virgin birth, when it became desirable to perpetrate that story. The gospel of Mark, which is the oldest gospel, has no pretention of a virgin birth tradition. Mark also does not mention the father of Jesus. Furthermore, the reference to Jesus, being the son of Mary in a gospel that does not have a birth narrative, must have been shocking and even scandalous. The gospel of Mark furthermore, seems to emphasize, and even dramatize the distance of Jesus from his family of origin, which ties into the scandal theory of the birth of Jesus, according to Mr. Spong.

Mr. Spong goes onto suggest the strong possibility that the gospel of John inserted symbolic language to a strong degree regarding the birth and other elements of the life of Jesus, in order to substitute for the literalism, which had projected itself in particular through the literal birth tradition. Although it may not have been intended, a consequence of this was the dehumanization of Mary with the elevation of her virginity status. The gospel of John also emphasizes the separation of Jesus from his brothers much as Mark did. Mr. Spong points out that the key evidence of the scandal of Jesus birth comes in chapter 8, where we have the insertion about the woman caught in the act of adultery, whom Jesus refused to condemn. Here Jesus uses the same word for woman that he did to address his mother in the wedding feast account. It is also in the midst of a heated debate and dialogue that occurs before this incident in John chapter 7 and continues later on in John chapter 8.

Over time the creeds of the church evolved to make more literal events attributed to Jesus. Once the reader has been thoroughly challenged with the concept of a virgin birth and removes the convenience of theology from much deeper meanings, John Shelby Spong then takes on the potential marriage of Jesus. He makes a strong case for Mary Magdalene. He notes that Mary Magdalene has priority in every passage that she has mentioned suggesting a potential relationship with Jesus. In fact, Mary Magdalene is the only name that all four of the gospels agree went to the tomb after the death of Jesus. Spong notes that the first miracle of Jesus of turning water into wine involves the mother of Jesus coming to him very concerned about they're not being enough wine. He raises the question of who would be troubled by this to the extent more than the mother of the groom , which would be Jesus himself.

Another story supporting Jesus being married, is the fact that the disciple Nathaniel calls Jesus rabbi for which a requirement in the first century Jewish culture would have been to be married. Mary Magdalene also makes a claim to the rights of Jesus body after death, which would only be appropriate if Mary Magdalene was the nearest of kin as in married to Jesus. Also, her use of the term my Lord was used in the same style that a Jewish woman of that era referred to her husband. Also recall the admonition of Jesus, for Mary Magdalene, not to hold him or embrace him after his death. First century Jewish women did not embrace or touch men, unless they were married and then only in private.

BORN OF A WOMAN – PART 2

Most of us are familiar with story of Mary and her sister Martha and the dinner that Jesus attends in their home. Martha is busy attending to the meal preparation and other domestic duties. Mary has chosen to spend time with Jesus in listening and conversation. In fact, we must not assume that it was a one-way street as Jesus could be a very effective listener himself. Martha is troubled about this and goes to Jesus for a corrective action plan. Jesus then points out that Mary has made a wise choice and may continue. This may well be Mary Magdalene, which name may be one derived by Mark, meaning large or magnificent. Experts note that contrary to what some think that there is no town of Magalene.

The point behind this process is not to make a sermon about this encounter which has been already sermonized plenty of times. Rather it is to point out that Jesus would only have had such authority that Martha is requesting in the Jewish society of that time, not because he was a male, but rather because he was the husband of this Mary, who some conjecture was Mary Magdalene. Indeed, as John Shelby Spong points out that such actions would be appropriate and only one of two scenarios. The first one was either Mary was his wife or the second was that she was a prostitute.

Despise Mary Magdalene has often been marginalized with hints that she was a prostitute, there is exactly zero evidence that she was indeed a prostitute. Luke notes that Mary Magdalene was a woman whom Jesus cast out seven demons but no other gospel supports this. Luke does mention a woman who is a sinner coming at night to Jesus, but does not identify her as Mary. John, on the other hand says that the woman was Mary, but the episode took place in her home with her sister, Martha and brother Lazarus. When John told his story, there is no hint of impropriety or sinfulness.

Nonetheless, it is almost as though there were a hidden agenda for Mary Magdalene to have some underlying major problems, such as prostitution, that would remove her place of priority. This person who has stood by Jesus side in life and death became replaced by the mother Mary. Mother Mary in turn, stood for virginity, and specifically virginity without ever having sex. It was therefore convenient to portray Mary Magdalene as just the opposite as someone who was a prostitute who had too much sex.

So, we have come full cycle to the renunciation process that happened. First we see the gospels having Jesus do a renunciation of his family, including to a degree his own mother. Over time, Mary Magdalene comes to be the stand in for mother Mary and her lost virginity, and has to undergo renunciation by having her be reconfigured as a prostitute. This leads to the renunciation first of sex in general, which is followed by the renunciation of the flesh by the church and all things in the flesh. Paradoxically the church, then circled back to mother Mary and gives her a most elevated status of veneration. She could only have this status though as long as she was sexless.

Spong makes his case that ultimately the symbol of the virgin becomes a weapon of male repression to women by defining them as less than males, and as a source of evil desire, for which women are guilty by virtue of being women. Strangely the suppression of such female energy was not a main feature of the Jewish culture of the time. The devil became associated with all things being renounced. Meanwhile, as the importance of the virgin rose, the status of women in general was lowered. Christianity chooses to ignore the fact that Paul appeared to know nothing of the virgin tradition when he wrote before any of the gospels were recorded. Likewise, the last gospel recorded of John does appear to deny the virgin tradition, or at least to set it aside.

BORN OF A WOMAN – PART 3 (THE MEANING OF CHRISTMAS)

We are accustomed to Christmas being about family time and getting together with perhaps a few friends included. We tell ourselves that it is not about the gifts, though at some level, most of us revert to our childhood and naturally recall healthy memories of gifts with family present. We then rationalize that the wisemen brought gifts and maybe the poor shepherds as well. We might have to use our imagination to conceive of the shepherds actually bringing gifts beyond themselves. After all, Christmas is supposed to be much ado about the imagination. We blend all of the gospel versions together to come up with our amalgam, but mostly the gospel of Matthew and the gospel of Luke.

We conveniently forget that Christmas begins with divorce in the gospel of Matthew. We might acknowledge that a rich ruler who did not like any opposition committed genocide, and even infanticide. Thank God, at least he did not do abortion. We also do not fully capture the fact that the wise man took a different route back to their own land rather than cater to the whims of a narcissistic ruler. These inconvenient truths are all contained in our gospels. Perhaps if we allow our imagination to expand when we start with the basic truths, we may have a different perspective.

We begin with the divorce that is mentioned in the first chapter of the gospel of Matthew. There we are told that Joseph was faithful to the law, and when he found out that his wife was pregnant, though not through him, he determined to divorce her quietly. Joseph appears to be an honorable man and was going to do this quietly, but again through the legal means. At this point, we must use only a little imagination to determine that his willingness to do so was an acknowledgment of forgiveness. After all, when he had made up his mind to divorce Mary quietly, he did not at that time know that the conception was from the Holy Spirit. Ultimately, we maintain that this is where Jesus learned about the birth of forgiveness. After all, it is the willingness to forgive even when we consider ourselves wronged, but even when the other person has done no wrong that we are able to ascertain

We tend to relish the role that angels play in the Christmas pageant. The angels appear to appear only to poor people. They bring good news, but they do not bring gifts. They appear to Mary and arguably to Joseph. They appear to the shepherds. Curiously, they do not appear to Jesus at his birth. It would appear that Jesus first encounter with angels is after he is tempted, humbled, and exhausted. Jesus will not see angels again until after he dies, humbled once again . Arguably angels come to us only after we are humbled and in significant need like the shepherds.

Next, we find the narcissistic ruler trying to wipe out all potential competition. Although he is a powerful man, he is fearful over little things, including children. After all, children not only have imaginations, but they have the uncanny ability to tell the truth. Notice that if the people cannot control the ruler and take measures into their own hands, then much unnecessary suffering occurs. There is a necessary displacement for safety. The God who has lit up the skies with angels to poor people has left the work for humans on this earth to do.

Indeed, both the shepherds and wise men return to their work. Contrary to what we often hear, the birth of a baby did not change the world. Rather, when that child grew up, he was filled with a forgiving spirit that was instilled in him before birth. He was nurtured in the ancient truths of his people and never forgot them. He transformed those truths into social action. You and I cannot stop a divorce which union does not have divine intervention. But we can minister to heal both parties. You and I can intervene when a narcissistic ruler threatens the wellbeing of children who need safety, shelter, and programs for improving their lives. Transformation is what made the 2024 movie the Best Christmas Pageant Ever so delightful. You and I cannot imagine any less of a transformation when we apply Jesus words of Mathew chapter 26: I was hungry and you fed me…….

Easter And The Women

We cannot tell the story of Easter without appealing to the role of the women involved. To be sure, the stories are going to vary not only in the synoptic gospels, but also in the gospel of John, which the scholars recognize having been written quite some time after the other gospels. We will begin with the gospel of Mark, which by all sources is indeed the most ancient gospel. There we are told that three women went to the tomb after the sabbath was over in order to anoint the body of Jesus.

To be sure, they, like everyone else who had witnessed the death of Jesus, believed Jesus to be dead. They believed, though that they still had a duty to anoint the body somehow recognizing that there is life that goes on as many ancient cultures recognized before modern physics also recognized that energy does not die. The women themselves very much respected the beliefs of their tradition, which was a major reason that they waited for the sabbath to be finished. This anointing appeared to be a woman's role and not that of a man in that era.

While they respected tradition, the women did not let obstacles such as a huge stone blocking the grave compromise their duty. To be sure they did not have faith that the stone would already have been moved. To be sure they did not have faith that Jesus was already risen, and that an angel would be sitting there to tell them. The reality, according to Mark, was what that the stone had been rolled away presumably by the angel, who is sitting in the tomb. We are told that the women, like any of us would be, were alarmed. Ironically the angel tells the women to not be afraid.

The angel is not instructing the women to be something that they are not, but rather to be something that is natural and helpful in a surprising situation. The women are given a brief narrative from the angel who recognizes that they are seeking Jesus who is crucified. The angel tells them that that Jesus has risen. Furthermore, they may see Jesus as he told them, by going to Galilee. The original version of Mark ends with the women still bewildered and living in fear. Because of this fear, they did not tell anyone in contrast to what they were instructed by the angel to do so.

An apparently later insertion in the story begins in verse nine of chapter 16 of the gospel of Mark. There we see that Jesus first appeared to Mary Magdalene, who was a woman Jesus had cast out seven demons. This time Mary determines to tell others, but they do not believe her. Later, Jesus will appear to two people walking in the country. They also tell the others, but once again, the others do not believe. Finally, Jesus appears to the remaining 11 disciples and rebukes them for their lack of faith and refusal to believe those who had seen Jesus after he had risen.

The gospel of Matthew has modified the story and notes that only two women went to the tomb. Here we are told that it is an earthquake that moved the stone, but also that guards were present who were placed at the request of the religious leaders of the community. The angel gives the same narrative story with the same command to not be afraid and to go tell the disciples of this great happening. On the way to the disciples these women are greeted by Jesus. For some reason, we have the insertion of the guards being paid off by the religious authorities. We feel it appropriate to acknowledge the story as entirely implausible for the soldiers to be paid off by the religious leaders, but rather itself also an insertion with strong anti-Semitic overtones. it is not only not essential to this gospel, but it is detrimental to the gospel wherever and whenever it is perpetrated.

The gospel of Luke begins on the first day of the week early in the morning. The initially unnamed women went to the tomb with concerns about the stone sealing the tomb, but this time finding the tomb open with two men inside instead of one. Those men ask why they were seeking the living among the dead. This time the women returned to tell the remaining disciples. Finally, we get their names. Once again, they are not believed although Peter feels that it is worth a chance to consider and runs to the tomb.

We then have an elaboration of the two men in the country from the gospel of Mark who become the men on the road to Emmaus. Jesus approaches them on the road but they do not recognize him. Jesus asks them to give an account of their dismay upon which the men tell the story of Jesus, being a powerful prophet who was crucified and was reported by women to be alive. Jesus then chides them for having missed the midrash connection with Scriptures. Jesus then stays with them at their invitation and breaks bread following which their eyes were opened. These believers return to Jerusalem to tell the disciples. In this gospel, they are the first human witnesses of Jesus after the resurrection. In this gospel, Jesus does not appear separately to the women, but appears next to the disciples.

In the gospel of John, we have only one woman going to the tomb, namely Mary Magdalene, who went while it was still dark. She finds the stone removed and runs to tell Simon Peter and the other disciple who was apparently John, that the body of Jesus is missing. When the two disciples get to the tomb, they find the burial clothes used for Jesus but this time no angel. In this gospel, Jesus appears first to Mary Magdalene. Mary then goes to tell the disciples.. Then Jesus appears to the disciples with the exception of Thomas who was not present in this account.

We can summarize all of these accounts, as needing at least one woman to be the bridge between the life of Jesus that they did not understand and the meaning, which was assigned to his death and resurrection after the various accounts. These accounts, according to John Shelby's Spong and his book on the resurrection are an attempt to shine meaning through midrash in which important events of the past are connected with later events to enhance both their importance and their meaning.

Essentially the story does not begin to happen or be told without the women. It is the women who are adhering to an ancient tradition both Jewish and international in terms of anointing the dead. One of the most believable parts of the earliest version along with the other versions is that the women were in fear. We are almost always fearful at the unexpected. It may be good news. The original story closes with the emphasis that they were so afraid that they did not even tell anyone. This leaves us with two possibilities. One is that the story was leaked out by them over time. The other is that over time various authors felt the need to enhance the original versions.

In the stripped-down version of the synoptic gospels it is women doing an ancient and religious custom of anointing the dead. They have very much respected the Jewish Sabbath and waited until it was completed. They have prepared spices for the body of Jesus. Yet they are unprepared as to how to roll away the heavy stone guarding the tomb. They are unprepared for angels. They are unprepared for an empty tomb. Even finding the tomb empty they are unprepared for a risen Jesus.

They are naturally in a state of fear. This is a major common theme in the synoptic gospels. The fear is not hidden. It is, borrowing from our medical profession, palpable. The angel or angels depending on the version, tell the women not to be afraid. This is not along the lines of Paul Tillich when he writes in his essay Be Strong, where he notes that we are not truly commanded to be something which we cannot be. To be sure the women continue to live in fear until it gradually dawns on them that what the angels had in mind was that living in fear was not consistent with their existential nature.

We maintain that the women had their own gradual eye opening much like the parallel story of the disciples on the road to Emmaus. It is after this point that they have the conviction along with the courage to tell others of concern what they had seen. Who Jesus appeared first to is irrelevant. The stories are not told for their historical accuracy but for their meaning. Accordingly, they can and indeed should vary. Variations indicate the intersection of human interpretation with divine events. Science which notes that an electron behaves like a wave at times and particle at other times gets that these seemingly incongruent energies both have partial truth that can only be meaningful when seen as a whole that is a paradox.

Each author gives the perspective in the resurrection story that they started their gospel with as we alluded to in our book entitled the Advent Style.. Different versions emphasize that Jesus appeared to different people first. That actually is not all that relevant. One can tell extreme slant in stories when someone feels compelled to add the anti-Semitic portion about the guards being bribed in the Matthew version . We will not apply anachronistic moralism to that reason which we can only conjecture. However, we will go so far as to say that any sermon or story that includes it has introduced a prejudice that is damaging. The good news for Matthew is that he closes as well with the great commission. The great commission is inclusive and universal. Furthermore, when Jesus says to teach people of all nations, they are indeed to obey everything that Jesus commanded the disciples. Those commandments very much appealed to adhering to the custom and religious practices that the disciples were already indoctrinated with.

We would do well to not lose sight of the fact that it was women following ancient religious traditions that existed in all ancient societies. They do not let great objects block their duty, even when they do not see an obvious or intellectual solution to the boulders of life. They are naturally afraid, as were Adam and Eve in the garden of Eden when they were confronted with a new way of thinking and a new paradigm. Fear kept the story to themselves. Ultimately they shared their story. When we are confronted with a new paradigm as the women were when they saw the empty tomb , and the men in white, it may be wise to acknowledge our fear and reflect and keep to ourselves for a time. It is no surprise that the story has become layered over with institutional interventions, with each serving its own particular purpose for the moment. Yet, within the original story is a truth that the ideas that represent a life that never dies, may themselves need to die, even as life goes forth in many expressions. The penetrating question of the angels for all time is why do we seek the living among the dead?

THE TRANSFORMATIVE POWER OF JESUS

Perhaps one of the most remarkable things about the gospels is the transformative power of Jesus. On his most basic level Jesus is able to see people as they truly are or even could be as opposed to how they have seen themselves or how society has perceived them. This is particularly evident in the healings of Jesus. It is no less so in the healing of women by Jesus, compared to the healing of men by Jesus. In some cases, Jesus goes to the individual. In some cases, the individual goes to Jesus and finally in other cases, the individual is brought by others to Jesus.

One of the great stories of someone going to Jesus by themselves is found in several of the gospels, including Mark chapter 5 in his most basic form where a woman was affected with hemorrhage for 12 years and had suffered greatly at the hand of many doctors and exhausted all her resources through them. Unfortunately, she only grew worse. She knew Jesus reputation though and sought to touch his clothes, knowing that this might affect a cure from her hemorrhage. Indeed, it did. It also provoked to response from Jesus when he sensed that healing energy had left his body. Since Jesus felt energy leave his body, we may presume that the healing physically had already occurred. Accordingly, The woman could have left well enough alone, since apparently Jesus really did not know who it was.

As it was, the woman realized that she had been healed physically, but knew that there might be more. She therefore declared the whole truth to Jesus. Jesus then provides the essential psychological assuredness that was part of the healing when he told her to go in peace and be cured. This implies permanency as opposed to what could have been possibly a temporary healing until the psychological aspect was recognized and pronounced. Now the woman would not have to look over her shoulder to wonder about a recurrence, but would be able to go in peace as the gospel notes.

The three synoptic gospels tell another story about a crippled woman who cannot stand erect. Her healing by Jesus occurs on the holy day. Her disability is attributed to a bad spirit. This woman had been crippled for 18 years. With this healing, Jesus is challenged by the religious authorities much as he is on other occasions when he heals men on the sabbath, including the gospel of John chapter 5, where he heals someone crippled for 38 years. That individual had camped out by a pool reported for its healing for those first responders to water movement. However, this poor individual had no one help him for 38 years until Jesus came along. The other example of a sabbath healing by Jesus is the blind man in John chapter 9.

Just like the healing of the woman who had to work to touch his coat, Jesus sometimes seems to require extra work for certain women and their healings. For example, the Syrophoenician woman begged Jesus to drive a demon out of her daughter. Jesus put her off with a little bit of a slur to challenge her intent. When the woman responded with courage, Jesus proceeded to perform the healing at a distance. Another foreign woman transformed by Jesus was the Samaritan woman who is asked by Jesus to give him a drink. The woman deflected Jesus request and statements before having a serious dialogue with him. This is highlighted by Jesus pointing out that he was indeed the Messiah that the woman had been talking about. The woman then proceeds to make a declaration of this connection to her friends, making one her one of the first to recognize Jesus as the Messiah as we read early in John chapter 4.

Perhaps the most poignant transformation occurs in the apocryphal story which begins at the end of John chapter 7. Indeed, many scholars feel that this story which had floated around in early Christianity is more fitting for the gospel of Luke. However, we describe it, it is certainly fitting of the philosophy of Jesus ministry. There in John chapter 8, we see a woman that has been brought to Jesus, having been caught in the act of adultery by the religious leaders. Their simple request is to have the law fulfilled and to have her stoned to death. Never mind that the male partner who is equally guilty is not present for this encounter.

Jesus knows full well that they are more interested in catching him than they are in stoning the woman. Jesus merely asks them to look into the stones known as their hearts. He is appealing to those leaders to look at their conscience and to determine how set in stone, like an idol that their hearts might be. Perhaps we have heard the story told so much that we have failed to acknowledge how readily those leaders were able to perform a 360° turn. Jesus then acknowledges those leaders' position in recognizing that there are consequences to sin for the woman herself. He instructs her to go and sin no more. Yet before we walk away ourselves from this story, we are meant to identify with someone in the story. Is it the leaders? The woman? Jesus? The rocks?

THE WOMAN WHO SAVED PAUL'S LIFE

We do not tend to think of the apostle Paul as one of our first choices for advancing the position of women. There may be lots of reasons for this, including not fully appreciating the historical context, but perhaps as much as any is people employing his name and attaching statements with that name that have become embedded as infallible scripture. Karen Armstrong has some nice insights in her book : Saint Paul the Apostle We Love to Hate. This essay will not reference that work much though the interested reader is highly encouraged to review her well researched work in order to have a better understanding of Paul in relationship to women.

The choice of Timothy as a protégé and colleague who was mentored by the apostle Paul is in large part due to the influence of Timothy's mother and grandmother as well documented. Meanwhile, a name that is overlooked despite being mentioned six times in the New Testament in the works of Paul, and the book of Acts is that Priscilla (Sometimes referred to as Prisca). She is typically mentioned with her husband Aquila. Most notable though is that four of the six references mention Priscilla first. Others have noted that this is no small concession, but rather a recognition of her greater prominence in the Christian community.

Notably, both Aquila and Priscilla were tentmakers like the apostle Paul. Accordingly, Paul stayed with them. They were also coworkers and missionaries who are knowledgeable about the Way. Ironically, they were expelled from Rome because of their Jewish connection while later the Apostle Paul diligently sought to be taken to Rome for justice. After these three individuals live together for a year and a half in the town of Corinth, they ventured together to Ephesus where once again they live together before Paul embarked on additional missionary journeys.

The expertise of Priscilla and Aquila in the Christian faith was exemplified when another expert named Apollos came to town as an authority on the Scriptures. He was said to be an eloquent and accurate speaker about Jesus, but his understanding was incomplete. Priscilla and Aquila took him aside to instruct him in the faith at a deeper level. With the mention of Priscilla's name first she appears to be the main tutor. This same Apollos returns to Corinth, where Priscilla and Aquila had left and has successful conversions arguing in public that Jesus was the Messiah.

Meanwhile, the apostle Paul returned from his mission work to and was reunited with Priscilla and her husband. The couple is named three more times in the Bible. While these mentions are brief, they are certainly suggestive of a close relationship to the apostle Paul. It would appear even that the church met at the house of Priscilla and Aquila. Notably Priscilla and Aquila stay on at Ephesus after Paul had to leave because of a riot over his teachings. This is a rather bold position by the husband and wife since the church was meeting at their house. When Paul sends greetings to them towards the end of Romans, he notes that, this husband and wife risked their life for him. This reference is given in Romans, chapter 16.

Another interesting facet of this chapter 16 of Romans is that there are 10 women mentioned. The significance is enhanced by the fact that while most of Romans is rather impersonal, chapter 16 is a reversal in contrast by being very personal. Some have suggested that this was a cover letter, and as such was actually indicative of a strong possibility of Priscilla and Aquila being back at Rome. This supports the ongoing boldness of the couple Priscilla and Aquila in relentlessly delivering the gospel under challenging or hostile circumstances. This daring approach along with saving the apostle Paul's life suggest that we look at his relationship to strong women with a deeper appreciation.

Mary And Martha Revisited

For this essay, I am indebted to the work women in the New Testament by Mary Ann Getty-Sullivan. Before you listen to another sermon or interpretation on the Mary and Martha interaction with Jesus, please review this or at least something that gives you the historicity of the event. You will appreciate a much more sophisticated interaction and exchange, then merely two women vying for the attention of Jesus with petty jealousy. This work will help to remove the palpable offense of inequity that we naturally feel when we hear the story.

Indeed, we do a significant injustice when we look at Mary as more favorable because she was listening to Jesus and not distracted by the work. Martha, on the other hand, seems to be distracted in her work and attempting to please Jesus. The elaboration of these themes is quite misleading unless we take in the historical context. The traditional telling of this story leaves an unsatisfactory taste in our mouth as we still feel a strong sympathy for Martha, who appears to be at least chided by Jesus to some gentle degree.

As Getty-Sullivan points out, one of Luke's concerns when he was writing in the eighth decade was in showing that being a Christian was not in conflict with the Roman ideals for women. Luke bent over backwards to be politically correct. Along these lines Luke demonstrates that Christian men and women were not only pious and respectful of tradition, but that they also practice standards for behavior as members of society that were well accepted. Mary approximates those standards and Martha threatens them.

Getty-Sullivan notes that the Pauline churches of the 50s may have been more able to afford the women prophets and teachers and apostles and deacons in their many untraditional roles, which is represented by Martha. By the time we get to Luke, we have a more domesticated church with Luke presenting Jesus as praising certain behavior in women in order for them to be models for others. These sisters represent a rift of the sisterhood of the early Christians. They were struggling with the more outspoken and action women of the earlier church of Paul as opposed to the traditional female role, appreciated by the Romans.

Getty-Sullivan presents an alternative consideration in which the women represent very different perspectives on the modes of discipleship in the first century that were interdependent. There was the opportunity to be like Paul in terms of charismatic and itinerant. By the same token there needed to be community who would have provided for the needs of such itinerant preachers. Accordingly, Martha may have represented the local hosts who provided the place and the support required by traveling missionaries. Mary, on the other hand, represents the itinerant preacher herself who moves from place to place. There would have been a natural tendency for there to be tension among the women just as we feel, in the way the story is presented in the gospel of Luke.

Before we pass too much judgment on Martha, we would do well to turn to the story told in the gospel of John chapter 11. There we see Martha making one of the first declarations that Jesus is the Messiah, the son of God. It is Martha who encounters Jesus first there upon the death of their brother Lazarus, and then proceeds to go and call Mary. The gospel of John tends to remove the tension between the two women. Mary's role to a large degree appears to introduce her for the preparation of the anointing to Jesus that she will do in the 12th chapter.

THE UPPER ROOM

Once again for this essay, we are indebted to the book women in the New Testament by Mary Ann Getty – Sullivan. As she notes the upper room had significance for the early believers. They formed a community to break bread and experience the resurrection symbolically. It is noted that the upper room was a domain typically considered as women's space. This space symbolized where the church would gather for many years. It was after all compatible with the community goals and formed the basis for a new society, which was based on the family. There was even a form of equality that seems to be dismissed over the years in terms of the role of men and women.

We may recall that Luke illustrates the origins of the church in the first chapter of Acts as spreading out from the closed doors of the upper room in Jerusalem. Even Mary, the mother of Jesus is present in the initial upper room in the first chapter of Acts awaiting the Spirit. Indeed, the unity of the disciples and other men with the women is recognized by Luke in that they were all of one accord in their devotion to prayer. In particular, the women form a link with the cross and the burial and the resurrection message for Luke's Gospel.

Women not only receive the Holy Spirit in the upper room in the book of Acts, but they are missionaries and witnesses in spreading the faith. They are also hosts of churches in their homes and teachers. They are beneficiaries of God's healing and the liberating power of such healing. All of this according to Clarice Martin also includes that they hailed from quite diverse economic backgrounds, including the very wealthy, but also economically disenfranchised.

While there is no one story that exemplifies the complete significance of the upper room, the story of Peter raising Tabatha, also known as Dorcas, from the dead illustrates many symbolic features. Luke mentions twice that this raising from the dead occurred in an upper room. This story is seminal in spreading the gospel outside of Jerusalem. A case can be made that Tabatha is referred to as a disciple and according to the research by Getty-Sullivan is the only woman so named in the New Testament.

Tabitha has a distinct track record of giving including clothing and other goods for the widows. There is also evidence that she had a strong influence outside of the feminine circle. Her raising from the dead by Peter has many similarities to the resuscitations from the dead that Jesus performed. Following this healing, the church begins to spread out notably into the homes of women and in particular to other upper rooms. This upper room represents the life giving benefits of the community of believers, and in particular the weekly memorial of the Lord's supper as signified by the breaking of bread.

Interestingly, the last reference to an upper room in the book of Acts is found in the 20th chapter. It is once again a resuscitation story this time by the apostle Paul. By this time in the book of Acts the role and work of Paul has supplanted that of Peter. Once again, this miracle is associated with a breaking of bread as a response to the miracle. Thus we see time and again the feminine place of the upper room being a place where life is restored without respect to gender or class.

Healing Women

The parable of the unjust judge found in Luke chapter 18 seems to set the tone for how Jesus approaches several of his healings and interactions with women. In the parable there is a poor widow woman who goes to the judge day and night to plead her cause. However, he will have nothing to do with her. She however is relentless and will not give up until she gets her justice. Finally, the judge says that he does not care about the woman or her cause, but he will give her what he wants in order to avoid being bothered by her further.

Some people may be offended that Jesus was comparing his own father God to the unjust judge. What he was really doing of course was setting the tone and standard for how hard we sometimes need to work and be persistent. In particular we believe that Jesus wanted to show a higher standard for females, but he recognized that they were going to have to work harder than men in order to receive their reward.

One of the classic examples that Jesus illustrated in real life is found in Luke chapter 8 starting with verse 40. In this stretch Jesus has been summoned by a ruler in order to heal his daughter. The set up here is Jesus responding to a rich male figure. A poor woman who has suffered with a bleeding disorder for 12 years tries to get close enough to simply touch Jesus's coat. With the crowd pressing in on him she sneaks up and secretly touches his coat and is instantly healed. Jesus turns around and asks very pointedly who touched him knowing that power had gone out from his body. When the woman is called out about the healing she comes trembling before Jesus only to ultimately be reassured and told to go in peace.

Perhaps a more dramatic example occurs in Matthew chapter 15 beginning with verse 21. There Jesus is solicited by a foreign woman crying out to have mercy on her. Jesus ignores her. His disciples, meanwhile, wish for Jesus to send the woman away, but he does not. Instead, he challenges this lonely foreign woman that she was not part of his mission. The woman does not seem to care what the original mission may have been. She simply replies, "Lord help me". He then gives her a further challenge noting that it is not right to take the children's bread and toss it to their dogs. She has a quick and clever response and knows that even the dogs eat the crumbs that fall from their master's table. (NIV). Ultimately, we have a poor foreign female who helps to define and even re-define the mission of Jesus by expanding it to foreigners as well as women. The harshness of Jesus testing of this woman was a reality of the challenges that both women and foreigners of the time were going to face.

NEW TESTAMENT PART 2

True Healing

Before leaving these two miracles of healing, we might ask the question of where does true healing originate. The combination seems to be one of some true internal scenes of faith such as the Mustard seed that Jesus talked about combined with a true source of healing, namely in this case Jesus. In the story of the woman with the hemorrhage we have an additional indictment in the version we found in Mark chapter 5. In the new international version, we read "she had suffered a great deal under the care of many doctors and had spent all that she had, yet instead of getting better she grew worse." (Mark 5: 26 NIV)

Let us return to another healing of a woman in which she will extend his challenge to the norms of his day with violating two of them at the same time. For this combination of healing return to the story found in Luke chapter 13 verses 10 through 16. In this setting we have the relatively young Jesus in his early 30s doing some teaching in the synagogue which itself would have been unusual for someone that young at that time. This time we do not have mentioned about the woman coming to Jesus but rather simply that she was there and had been crippled by the spirit for 18 years.

In this setting Jesus approaches her and says to her that she is freed from her infirmity, and she is healed on the spot. The leader proceeds to remind Jesus rather indignantly that he has violated a healing by doing this on the Sabbath. Jesus then reminds them with a rather practical example of what they would do for their own animals on the Sabbath. He then points out the woman's connection both with

Abraham, indicating that this is a Jewish woman on one hand, and the foothold on her well- being by Satan.

Let's turn our attention to other encounters with women by Jesus that do not necessarily involve a physical healing. We have already discussed the interaction with Mary and Martha and the way that he elevates the status of women in that situation.

Another encounter in which she will elevate both the status of women, foreigners, and sinners is the story found in John chapter 4. This is the story of the woman at the well to whom Jesus asks for a drink of water. When the woman points out that she is a Samaritan to whom Jewish people especially men like Jesus tend to avoid interactions with. Jesus once again points out the original mission of God for the Jews and then surprises her with his awareness of the interaction that she has had with men which is plentiful. This encounter has both measures of direct confrontation and awareness as well as subtleties that may go unnoticed. Jesus accepts this woman with her background, and all was without either condoning her sin or condemning it. This combination liberates her to the point that she wishes to tell many others about it even though it will involve a public confession of the challenged life that she has had.

This story is reminiscent of the sinful woman who washed Jesus's feet during an important dinner. One of the major importance's of the story is that it is one of the few that is found in all four Gospels. Notably it occurs in Matthew chapter 26 shortly after the judgment day parable in which Jesus commends the righteous who attended people in need regardless of their background. While there has been much speculation and conflation about the background of this woman, we recommend the book Born Of A Woman by John Shelby Spong to further explore this concept.

Finally, there is arguably no story that is more poignant than the apocryphal story told at the start of John chapter 8. This is the story about the woman caught in the act of adultery and brought by the Jewish leaders for Jesus two other of his verdict as well. In this drama Jesus turns the table on them and asks that he who is without sin to throw the first stone. After the men have departed one by one, Jesus turns to the Woman and asks where her accusers are. He then proceeds to note that neither does he condemn her but rather that she is to go in peace and sin no more. Spong also has a nice expose about this story as well.

WOMEN IN HIGH AND LOW PLACES

This section will attempt to cover stories not previously mentioned in out other features on women. There is no particular cohesion here other than all of the stories support roles for women in unique ways. Let's start with the high places and review the argument for women as disciples. The most telling story comes from Jesus mouth as he is concluding a confrontational chapter with the religious authorities on healing on the sabbath, healing demon possessed and blind in Matthew chapter 12. With the placing in proper perspective of the law, Jesus has simultaneously demonstrated when it is appropriate to suspend that law or place it in context.

The question arises if there is a setup for the elevation of women. Let's use Matthew as our model for this discourse since that is where the first key example resides. In Matthew we have a series of generic healings unidentified people that occur after the temptations Jesus. Then we have the interlude of the Sermon on the Mount. We almost begin to see faces in Matthew chapter 8 when we have first a leper who was healed and then next the son of a centurion. Still nothing really identifiable here. The first full identification for a healing is no less than the mother-in-law other disciple Peter. A female of course. Jesus is not merely giving sight to the blind, speech to the mute, calmness to the wild and crazy, movement to the paralyzed but recognition to women.

Chapter 12 of Matthew takes this the next step by pointing out the role of women at women at a level beyond healing. First of all, to silence the attacks of a religious right who sought to control Jesus, we have a reference by Jesus involving people of a non-Jewish background who became significant believers. This was no less than the story of Jonah who preached to and converted the men of Nineveh after God had pledged to destroy the city. So much is made of the 3 days in the belly of a huge fish, just as Jesus was going to be in a darkness of similar proportions and beyond. In so doing we may obscure the role of women we believe that this whole section is leading up to. Jesus will reference the Queen of the South as coming to hear the wisdom of Solomon and then note that something greater than Solomon was there.

We have the recognition of the sign of Jonah when arguably the bigger sign there was the foreign believers. We have the Queen of the South with reference to something greater and the obvious answer seems to be Jesus. Yes, but. The next human encounter is with Jesus addressing the crowd while someone tells him that his family of origin is there to see him. He asks a rhetorical question of who is his mother and brothers. Then he points to his disciples and says that these are his mother and brothers. He would not have made this statement about women without women being among his disciples. Echoes of this occur in Luke chapter 8 where women were named supporters of the ministry. Jesus is greater than Solomon not simply because of his wisdom but also the action that takes in women as disciples.

Women Uplifted

Jesus liked the example of women such that he had key references and stories built around them. He tells the parable of the leaven with a female perspective to represent how such a small amount of positive change could affect the whole batch. The ten virgins are meant to be a positive example of females doing watchful waiting for the Master. Perhaps one of the hidden gems is in the parable of the lost coins found in Luke chapter 15 right after the more famous one lost sheep out of a 100 and right before the story of the Prodigal. We are meant to hear the role of women in preserving what is important by going out of their way to find and preserve that which they value, which puts them on par with a lowly shepherd looking for the one lost sheep or the Prodigal where the father does not even go looking.

In real life Jesus will challenge women and uplift them at the same time. Take for example the healing of the foreign woman in Matthew chapter 15 and Mark chapter 7. The woman has a possessed daughter and seeks healing. Jesus notes that such is reserved for God's chosen race, the Jews. Jesus chides her and make reference to her race being like dogs. So, let's not miss the setup here. Foreigner, woman, daughter with mental illness. Jesus knows if such a woman is going to survive that she has to be tough and tested. No doubt Jesus senses this and realized that his challenges, representing what the woman actually dealt with on a day- to-day real way, would be recorded for antiquity as a positive message about such.

In the kingdom of heaven, no talent or gift is too small. Once again like the mustard seed or the leaven, a little bit goes a long way. Such is the poor widow's offering cited in Mark chapter 12 and Luke chapter 21. Jesus says that this woman has given more than all the others because they gave out of their abundance and she out of her poverty. Like the woman who touched his garment, women do not need to do much to yield great impact.

From the time Jesus performs his first miracle which is for a woman, (whom he also makes work for the miracle, even though it is his own mother.) until the resurrection where Jesus first appears to a woman, we see the role of women as inextricably bound up with the message of Jesus.

Parable Gender Part 1

In this section we will explore the concept of which gender may have had the biggest influence on influence on the recording of a parable. We acknowledge taking acknowledge taking some great liberties in speculation here but believe that many will find the exercise fruitful for their own reflection. In so doing we recognize that there were followers of Jesus who were men as well as followers who were women as is recorded in the scriptures. We also accept the commonly researched and historically supported beliefs supported beliefs that the gospels were not recorded until quite some time after the life and in person teachings of Christ. Therefore, oral tradition would have kept these important stories alive. Our method here will be of dialogue back and forth as to our speculation on which gender was the most likely to have kept the story alive. Basically, there will be 4 categories: 1) predominantly transmitted by male influence. 2) predominantly transmitted by female influence. 3) Could have been either. 4) Clear elements of both.

Steve: Let's begin with the Parable of The Growing Seed found in Mark 4:26-29.

Rich: We need to keep in mind that simply because the main character is a male does not mean that the story was kept alive predominantly by men.

Steve: This is true, but I think in this case we can agree that this story would have been perpetuated by mostly men. We have a man planting seed which would have been overwhelmingly men in those days. Then like today's sitcom man he sits back and does nothing while the seed grows on its own. Finally, he gets active again at harvest time.

Rich: Seems obvious. Let's keep in mind the counterpoint that there is a fair amount of watchful waiting, and patience involved that often reflects the feminine perspective.

Steve: True, and I think females would have also emphasized the constant nurturing of the crops.

Steve: OK. Let's turn to our next parable: The Parable of Two Debtors found in Luke 7:36-50. I like this story because of the poignancy told at a real live event where Jesus is the guest for dinner at a religious leader's house. A woman who has led a sinful life washes the feet of Jesus with perfume and tears while the religious leader looks on in disgust and judgement.

Rich: Here I have to feel that this story was perpetuated by women, and not merely because the main character was a woman but also because of the role that she plays.

Steve: I agree. The parable itself though involves only women. However, it does not have some of the harsh male overtones about debt that some other parables have.

Rich: Let's look at the parable of the Lamp Under a Bushel found in Matthew 5: 14-15, Mark 4:21-25, Luke 8: 16-18. I like the Sermon on the Mount version in Matthew because it pairs the parable with the Light of the World. As a household metaphor, I have to favor women telling this story.

Steve: I agree. Only Luke mentions gender which he credits to male. Still with the domestic influence was one likely kept alive predominantly by women. It has elements of the hidden in Mark which uncommonly has the most elements for a synoptic story. I think Luke may have wanted the male influence but that the more original story in Mark is a rare version of being longer and expansive. It allows for the exposure and expressions of things previously hidden such as the female perspective.

Rich: Let's look next at the parable of The Good Samaritan. I think this outreach was one of overcoming prejudice. In the story of the parable itself it is about race or ethnicity, but I think women likely latched on to this and felt it applied to their gender as well.

Steve: I agree. Although all the characters are male there. is a strong feminine sensitivity. Males of course may be sensitive, but I think the context of told live when a lawyer was asking Jesus about who his own neighbor was expanded on by Jesus to be more inclusive. Curiously, we are not told the gender of the men who did the beating of the individual, but I can't imagine anyone listening to this who does not think of men and testosterone doing the deed.

Rich: Unfortunately, there are certain stereotypes that we can't escape. The elements of making sure that this stranger who dresses the wounds immediately are strongly feminine. Let's not forget the male influence here where the Samaritan hero puts himself in harm's way without second thought, much like a traditional male military hero. Testosterone may have its presumed downside in this story, but it also has its redemption.

Steve: Good point.

Parable Gender Part 2

Steve: The next Parable is the Parable of the Importunate Neighbor Luke 11: 5-8. This seems pretty straightforward. Men might ignore their friends and neighbors for a spell, but women never would.

Rich: Yes, but one that it is often compared with, namely the Persistent Widow or Unjust Judge in Luke 18:1-8 seems too, very feminine. A woman who knows what she wants and won't give up until she gets it.

Steve: Even more I like the fact that Jesus is using a female figure to confront a male who represents God. We all get that Jesus was persistence but the audacity to use a female confront the Godlike symbol. One of those probably not fully appreciated then or today. Certainly a 10 on the Richter scale for the times.

Rich: Next, we have the parable of the Rich Fool in Luke 12:16-21. Seems to be classic male greed for a story told in response to a question about male inheritance.

Steve: I agree. As we have pointed out elsewhere, he may also have been lazy and presumptive.

Steve: Next, we return to the Sermon on the Mount for the parable of the Wise and Foolish Builders found in Matthew 7:24-27 as well as Luke 6:46-49. My initial impression for the times is that it is about construction and told by males according to the builders of the times.

Rich: I agree although women may have appreciated the unmovable aspect. They also would have warned about the shortcut perils.

Rich: Let's look at the parable of New Wine into Old Wineskins in Matthew 9:14-17, Mark 2:18-22, and Luke 5:33- 39. The live background is at a banquet which setting Jesus was known to challenge social norms. Accordingly, I think women kept this story going.

Steve: I think that is healthy thinking.

Steve: Doesn't seem like much argument for the parable of the Strong Man or Parable of the Burglar in Matthew 12:29, Mark 3:27, and Luke 11: 21-22.

Rich: Seems straightforward. The inner beauty is that Jesus can compare himself to a thief.

Rich: The parable of the Sower seems to play off of traditional male farming and all the things that can go wrong.

Steve: For me this could be a mixture because the seed is sown everywhere indicating inclusion.

Steve: I don't have a good feel for the parable of the Tares or Weeds in Matthew 13:24-30 where the servants were warned to let the weeds grow right along the good seed until harvest so as to destroy the good.

Rich: Could go either way but a woman would never be comfortable with a a bunch of weeds among good plants.

Steve: Yes perhaps this is related to the Parable of the Fig Tree found in Luke 13:6-9. In this parable the main male figure wants to tear down a tree that has not borne fruit. Another voice which I think represents the feminine. pleads for one more year to heal itself.

Rich: Let's look at the Parable of the Mustard Seed in Matthew 13:31-32, Mark 4:30-32, and Luke 13:18-19 and compare it with the parable of Leaven in Matthew 13:33 and Luke 13:20-21. We have the leaven being traditionally for the female cooking.

Steve: At the same time, we have the mustard seed planted likely by males. I think these stories were paired for Jesus to get the attention of both sexes back-to-back.

Steve: Let's look at the Parable of the Pearl in Matthew 13:45-46 alongside the parable of Hidden Treasure in Matthew 13:44. To me this represents the feminine side depicted in the lost coins story in Luke 15:8-10. Rich: perhaps much like the parable of Drawing in the Net in Matthew 13: 47-52 which is very proximate to others above. It represents inclusion.

Rich: You know I like to reflect on the cost of discipleship and so will take the lead on the Counting the Cost parable in Luke 1428-33. Seems to be mostly a male perpetuation.

Steve: I agree as the concept of hating family does not seem to be something that would flow out of the feminine aspect.

Parable Gender Part 3

Steve: Let's turn to the parable of the Pharisee and Sinner or Tax Collector in Luke 18:9-14. Seems like this could go either way. Ultimately male machismo is put in its place and the humble are uplifted. Accordingly, I have to favor the feminine.

Rich: Yes, especially since it is paired with the unjust judge parable.

Rich: I think we have a slam dunk for the parable of Vineyard Workers in Matthew 20:1-16. Men could not keep a story extant that has this much work imbalances, etc. Steve: I agree. This story would have quickly died without women.

Steve: I think the same thing with the parable of the Two Sons in Matthew 21:28-32. The first son when asked by the father said he would not work but actually preceded to do the work whereas the second son said sure on the work but didn't do it.

Rich: If the father couldn't get the second son to move, say he goes to the wife for help and gets it.

Rich: The parable of the Wicked Husbandmen in Matthew 21:33-41, Mark 12:1-9, and Luke 20:9-16 seems so harsh as to be nothing less than male vengeance.

Steve: The violent theme is palpable to borrow from the medical jargon.

Steve: The parable of the Great Feast in Matthew 22:1-14 and Luke 14:15-24 serves as the antithesis for women. The invited guests have shunned the wedding and must be taught a lesson.

Rich: Yes, women demonstrate hospitality and reaping the rewards.

Steve: The version in Luke focuses on not choosing the honored seat at the wedding in order to not be embarrassed. Guys would drink such adjustments off while women would never forget it.

Rich: The parable of the Budding Fig Tree found in Matthew 24:32-35, Mark 13:28-31 and Luke 21: 29-33 does not seem to give much clue as to which sex would have kept this alive. Steve: I agree by itself, but if paired with the barren fig tree we mentioned earlier we see some feminine overtones but could go either way.

Steve: What about the parable of the Lost Sheep? To me this is part of the triad in Luke chapter 15 about the Lost. This part of the triad of lost seems the top layer of a sandwich where this is the top layer with male influence predominantly.

Rich: Yes, and the lost coin for women in the middle with the Prodigal being the bottom layer of the sandwich.

Steve: Yes, as powerful as the Prodigal is, we have no mention of the mother or other feminine perspective.

Rich: The parable of the Unforgiving Servant 18:21-35 seems to be another example of male vengeance. Steve: Yes, what female would have kept alive a story where the entire household paid the price for the male's transgressions.

Steve: The female antithesis of the above seems to be found in the parable of the Unjust Steward in Luke 16:1-13. To me this is a business savvy response that isn't fair in the male world but is demonstrating the power of negotiation. Rich: Yes, the male world would never reward this or keep the story alive.

Rich: The Rich Man and Lazarus is our next parable found in Luke 16:19-31. This parable illustrates that there comes a time when it is too late to repent. That does not sound like a feminine perspective.

Steve: I agree in general. It is, by the way, the only parable with someone with a name which could be a faint hint of the feminine.

Steve: I think our next parable of the Master and Servant in Luke 17:7-10 could go either way.

Rich: Some might misread this anachronistically as female subservience, but that is not really what it is about. It is about subservience to the kingdom.

Rich: The parable of the Door Keeper in Matthew 24:42-51, Mark 13: 34-37, and Luke 12:35-48 seems open to speculation.

Steve: Yes, even Peter who was present for the original story wondered who the parable was for. Jesus seems implying that it is for everyone.

Steve: Is the parable of the 10 Virgins in Matthew 25: 1- 13 automatically feminine?

Rich: While main character gender does not necessarily translate into who kept the story line intact, it does seem to be the case here. There is however the exclusion of the foolish virgins which goes a little against this.

Steve: I think this is all part of an elaborately orchestrated chapter in Matthew 25 where we have the first parable as the feminine. Then we have the parable of the Talents which is predominantly masculine. The conclusion is the parable of the sheep and goats which shares fairly equally elements of both.

Rich: Indeed, with the Talents we have a harsh taskmaster who starts off with an unequal distribution of talents. Then on his return he seems very demanding. Finally, he compensates once again in a very unequal manner. Women would not retell that story.

Steve: The chapter concludes with the end times sheep and goat's parable. We have here a king who rewards the unsuspecting dispenser of common every day good deeds. The perfect blend really.

Steve: The parable of the shrewd manager seems at first glance to be so full of male double crossing that it would have been kept alive by men. Of course, we don't stop with the first look approach.

Rich: Yes, plus in those times would men have perpetuated a story where a man goes against the boss, and then rewarded for it? This has some collaboration to it that suggests female relationship building. This is "mom" coaching the "dad" before he really messes up.

Steve: To me it makes it a mixed story. The man acknowledges with typical male pride that he is too ashamed to beg. By the same token, how many guys in those days would have said that they were too weak to do a physical occupation?

Rich: Our intentions must reflect our choice, "Which master do I serve"? That choice will reveal our intentions and determine our actions.

WOMEN AND UNION WITH GOD AS SEEN IN PARABLES

In one of our earlier works, entitled, Parables and Paradox, we discussed speculatively, which parables may have been perpetuated by which gender. We have included that section in this book. Our purpose here is to look at the rather limited parables in which women figure prominently. We might consider the parable of the lost coin. There a woman has some coins, but noticed that she has lost one. She works diligently to find the lost coin. Behavior economics would point out that a lost coin may have more perceived value than a coin that we either earned or found. Typically, we might think of such a parable as one of a rather poor woman who very much needed this coin. However, others have pointed out that she is a woman of agency and like any business person of either sex, merely wishes to protect that which is her own again as behavior economics would predict.

Of course, we are told that this is a part of the trio of the lost. This trio occurs in the 15th chapter of Luke and begins with the hundred sheep and the one sheep that was lost and sought out. Then it is narrowed down to the 10 for which one is lost and sought out. Then it is narrowed down to the two as in the prodigal in which the prodigal returns. As we have noted elsewhere, though there are no overt visible efforts by the father to seek out the prodigal. Rather, the father believes enough in the independence of the son to allow him to sew his seed, perhaps figuratively and literally in a foreign land. We might imagine that the father prays day and night for his son, and yet that father is seemingly surprised when he sees the son on the horizon and runs out to meet him.

We then have the parable of the 10 virgins at the feast. We will turn to Matthew chapter 25 for this parable as there are several other major parables that play off of a theme. The theme is somewhat the theme of the unexpected. In the first parable, we have the 10 virgin's half of whom are wise and half of whom are foolish. Because of the delay in the bridegroom's arrival, the five foolish virgins were out of the oil to keep their lamps lit. Notably, the five wise virgins would not share their oil. In fact, the five foolish virgins are locked out of the celebration feast. The next story in the same chapter is the parable of the talents. In somewhat of an unexpected twist, those who have the most end up even getting more. This even has been called the Matthew effect. Finally, we have the classic sheep and goats' story in which once again the unexpected happens for those who do not recognize that people in need represent Jesus himself. This chapter represents men and women, rich and poor and protecting one's own interests in contrast with that of providing for those that cannot.

In Matthew chapter 13, we read about one of the potential most authentic parables that Jesus told according to the Jesus seminar. This is the story of how the kingdom of heaven is like yeast that a woman took and mixed into many pounds of flour which worked its way all through the dough. This is paired up with two parables that are clearly male oriented about the parable of the sower, and then the parable of the weeds. Although the chapter parables flow lock step, the women parable with the flour does not get any explanation, unlike the men's parable of the sower. Perhaps Jesus knew that women would get this basic parable right away. The point throughout the chapter seems to be that a little bit can go a long way in terms of the truth and its influence.

The gospel according to Thomas talks about a parable attributed to Jesus as the woman with a jar. Although it is a non-canonical gospel, the Jesus seminar gave a pink rating meaning that in their opinion, it was probably an authentic saying of Jesus. The seminar noted that in that gospel, it is paired with the mustard seed parable and the parable of the leaven in which in all three cases there is something either unnoticed or unexpected, which occurs. Many scholars feel that the emptying of the jar reflects the need to empty ourselves unexpectedly in order to experience the kingdom. By the same token, we all leave a trail behind us that we may not know about.

Another strong female image is found in saying number 75 of the gospel of Thomas. There Jesus says that there are many standing at the door, but it is the solitary one who will enter the bridal chamber. Giles in his book Quantum Sayings of Jesus points out at this represents the single solitary integrated whole person who may enter the kingdom. He notes as we see above, that the bridal chamber is a common reference for the kingdom of God and also that it suggests the ultimate intimacy with God as when a husband knows his wife on the wedding night and they become the metaphorical one flesh. He notes that this is alluded to in the gospel of John where John says "now this is eternal life to know God and his son. The word Ginosha is the Greek word here in which knowing represents the type of intimacy reserved for those having the full intimate sexual experience. It is the vivid image of the intimacy experience between flesh and spirit and is the ultimate power of transformation.

You have to love a divinity who uses this rich metaphorical imagery to represent God with imagery of men and women, rich and poor in the most intimate of images.

Mark From Advent To Resurrection

This book began with the premise that we felt the stories and styles of each Gospel would be a reflection of the tone set in the Advent story. We believe that that tone is indeed reflected in the original resurrection story in the Gospel of Mark. For Mark that would appear to be a cut to the chase version. Verse one of chapter 1 of the Gospel of Mark will both identify Jesus as the Messiah as well as the son of God.

The second verse in the Gospel of Mark will connect Jesus with the Original Testament prophet Isaiah and set the tone for repeated connections with the Original Testament throughout the gospel. As an editorial note consider employing the term Original Testament as a replacement for every time you either read or think of the term or phrase Old Testament. That simple change may enhance the connection between the God of yesterday and today and tomorrow.

Please consider Jesus own words that he had not come to do away with the law and the prophets. Rather he was both an extension and fulfillment. A re-reading of the Gospel of Mark with the parables and the healings and the encounters with the religious leaders may reveal some additional perspective for the original intent.

Even the resurrection story in the Gospel of Mark has elements of respect for the Original Testament along with the new perspective. Mary Magdalene and the other women respected the original Sabbath before their visit to the tomb. Their expectations were to find a dead body of someone that they had been close to. Their intent was to perform Original Testament rituals for that loved one.

It was that devotion to the Original Testament rituals that was able to overcome their puzzlement as to how the large stone had been rolled away from the grave site. Their expectations and surprise could not be assuaged by one with an angelic appearance. They came out of duty and devotion and left in fear and disbelief. Despite being told that Jesus had risen and would be seen by them, they did not believe it.

The original conclusion notes that they told nothing to anyone because they were afraid. Our goal is not to challenge the additional story added to the Gospel of Mark even though various elements are clearly not in the style of the rest of the book. Clearly the women ultimately experienced Jesus and spread the message.

For modern believers we may take heart that the ultimate truth cannot be suppressed because of our fear and lack of faith. Sometimes we will find that rituals which connect us with our original understanding of the truth will get us through the day. When we are open to the source of truth that can roll away our fears, we may be exposed to a bright light that we will never understand completely but can always appreciate.

Resurrection Summary

We began our introduction on Advent by noting that there were four basic styles giving people their choice of approach to the Gospels. At some level those four Gospels not only represent differences but could actually be presented in such a manner that they were not in conflict with each other. That challenge is more difficult with the story of the resurrection.

This becomes a problem only if one is fixated on the actual words and stories as opposed to the meaning behind the stories. Our purpose here is to illustrate what they have in common and the strengths that each one has as well as how the style of advent relates to the style of the resurrection. Ultimately the gospels all have something that points far beyond the grave and is motivation for the living.

All of the Gospels involve women going to the tomb first. Three of the gospels have Jesus encountering women first. Interestingly only Luke, who seems to have a preference for women over men in the advent story, does not have Jesus appearing to a woman first. Rather in the Gospel of Luke he appears to strangers and himself remains undisclosed to them during that journey encounter.

We are told however that the most reliable manuscripts available for the original gospel namely Mark do not contain any actual appearances of Jesus with the original conclusion. Rather the original ending ends abruptly with fear. If it is true that Matthew and Luke borrowed heavily from the ancient Gospel of Mark, then the writer who concludes the Gospel of Mark likely reciprocated and borrowed elements from both of those gospels.

All of the gospels ultimately have Jesus appearing to the disciples and giving them promises and commissions to fulfill. The bonus section of Mark includes the commission to go into the world and preach the good news to everyone. It is emphasized that the believers will be able to do various miracles. Just as the opening chapter of Mark includes baptism and driving out demons so too does the expanded conclusion. In addition the first appearance of Jesus in Mark is to a woman previously demon possessed.

In Matthew when Jesus appears to the disciples he gives them the great commission to go in the world and baptize people in the name of the father and the son and the Holy Spirit and to teach them to obey everything he has commanded. In John Jesus ultimately gives the Holy Spirit and the power of forgiveness to the disciples. In Luke Jesus gives the disciples repentance and forgiveness and will send them what God promised which is apparently a reference to the Holy Spirit.

In summary we have four Gospels with four important gifts. These gifts include baptism which like Advent shares the concept of new birth. The next gift is that of the call for repentance. John the Baptist and the Original Testament prophets had it correct in that there can be no growth without turning away from something and turning towards something different. Because we may be very attached to what we are trying to turn away from, forgiveness is essential.

When it is all said and done the four Gospels point to the one remaining and unifying gift of the Holy Spirit. This unifying and eternal gift allows a person to be born again and inspires them to repent and to turn in to what they can be. Most importantly it confers for people the courage to forgive when forgiveness would seem humanly impossible.

WOMEN WITH QUESTIONABLE BACKGROUNDS

ALL IN THE FAMILY

While it is easy to fall into anachronistic judgement of some past societal values, it may be just as much problematic to be dismissive of certain actions without probing their relevance. Our case in point is that of intimate relationships with close family members and the portrayal of those interactions. We have already referenced two such occasions where Abraham tries to pass his wife off as his sister, in order to save his own skin. One can argue that indeed Sarah was his sister and even that she was his sister before she was his wife. But that would be distorting several measures. It would be obscuring the fact that it is only a half-sister by virtue of sharing the same father but not the same mother. Next it would be prioritizing the relationship of family of origin over that of the role of partner. Many of us might consider our partners as our best friend. Most of us who do so would not tend to introduce that partner as our best friend as opposed to an introduction as our partner.

Where the story really begins is in the first chapter that we are introduced to Abraham in Genesis 11. There what is not mentioned may be as important as to what is mentioned. There is no mention there where Sarah is introduced to us that she is related to Abraham in any way, shape, or form. One exception is The Living Bible. Why the omission? Why the emphasis on the fact that she is barren to the exclusion of her other relationship to Abraham as sister. Why do we get more information about Abraham's brother's relationships including women and genealogy than we do about Sarah? No doubt there is a fair chance that a first reading in chapter 11 will confirm what you might have recalled earlier from Sunday School, namely that one of Abraham's brothers, Haran, had died but had a son named Lot who resides under the domain of Abraham. What may not be so obvious is that Abraham's other brother Nahor married that deceased brother's daughter.

Now biblical students may recall the New Testament story where the religious leaders try to pinpoint Jesus about the afterlife and family connections. They point out the law of Moses which noted that a brother was to marry his brother's widow in order to carry on the family linage. If 8 brothers subsequently died, whose wife would the widow be in the afterlife. This is however, a different situation with Abraham and his family. Our real point here though is why no mention of the other relationship that Sarah has towards Abraham. Later on we will see that Abraham wants to send his trusted servant back to Abraham's native land to secure a wife for his son Isaac, from among his own kin. A lengthy chapter is indeed devoted to this story. In hindsight it is easy because of his other associations to be judgmental of Lot who had intercourse with both of his daughters when drunk by them, but is that process so far removed from others that seem less notorious? The Lot-daughters incident is referenced elsewhere. Later, we will see other offspring of Abraham pursuing some version of the all in the family process.

HAGAR, SEEN BY GOD

Hagar is the penultimate symbol for much that is oppressed. She is after all, a rejected female who is disposable after she has been used for her purpose. She represents the dark skinned, foreign woman who belongs to a rich woman who abuses her and then is discarded by the rich husband after he has had his way with her. She is the alien homeless pregnant female who is about to become the welfare mother. She is the young runaway while simultaneously representing the divorced woman without resource. Ironically, she is an Egyptian lady who is being castigated by a woman who the Egyptians themselves wanted to take advantage of. For that part of the story, we return you to Genesis chapter 12 where Abraham tries to pass off his beautiful wife Sarah as merely his sister. The ruse is ultimately discovered when calamity strikes the Pharaoh who is trying to take advantage of Sarah.

This whole prelude to what happens next to Hagar seems to be one of the greatest miscarriages of justice. The country of Egypt has taken in Abraham during a famine and dealt with his deceptions. It is quite possible that Hagar was a token given to Abraham after the deception event recounted above. The faithful Egyptian slave girl, Hagar, has done her duty, and had relations with an older man only to face abuse that was egregious enough to cause her to go into the desert in the gravid state without any seeming provisions. Then there is the encounter with the angel of the Lord in the desert. There are several notables about this brief encounter. First, as often happens God calls on a person by using their name and their position, Hagar, servant of Sarah. Next, he asks the rhetorical question of where has she come from and where is she going. This question, like those God poses to us, is to orient ourselves and not God.

Next Hagar aligns herself with God's description and says that she is indeed the servant girl or slave of Sarah and is running away. She does not list her reasons why as she perhaps figures that someone who knows that much about her could discern her reasons for leaving. She might further discern the next step, namely that God would protect her even as she is returning to the same hostile environment. She could not remotely predict that God would give her a blessing and make her the matriarch of many descendants, even if those descendants were to live in strife. But are there things that even God cannot see coming?

Before we address this, we return to the transition of the recognition of God that happens frequently in the Original Testament. In this progression, God presents first as the Angel of the Lord, only to transition later in the same passage to the actual Lord. There is a vague semblance of this in Genesis chapter 18 where we have the mention of 3 men who present to Abraham, with the realization ultimately that one of them is the Lord. In that scenario The Lord turns to consult his fellow companions for advice. There are remnants of this approach with the angels who appear to Lot with the strong suggestion that the Lord God is one of them before it is all said and done. These subtle presentations give way to a more revealing sequence when Abraham goes to sacrifice his son Isaac, and appears first as the angel of the Lord during the intervention phase and then once again, transitions into the full Lord phase. This way of thinking comes to its culmination when Jacob has his first dream of God. There the angels of God lead directly to God.

So now we have the stage set for Hagar to serve as a prototype for one who is first approached in a subdued fashion or disguise, only to be revealed ultimately as the Lord God. Furthermore, she is the prototype of one wandering in the desert. She has the distinction of wandering in the desert on 2 separate occasions well before Moses. She serves as a role model for Joseph for him to get through his forsaken experience in the desert. These experiences are not lost on Joseph, much like other relatives experiences he will capitalize on. So that the link may be completed, Joseph marries an Egyptian woman after falsely being accused by another Egyptian woman of wealth and status.

There are other revelations that may be lost upon us that are both subtle and profound. For example. God makes direct pledges to Abraham about his offspring as well as to give him the metaphors of dust and sand and stars which are too numerous to count. Yet nowhere does God give a direct mention to anyone except Hagar that her descendants will be too numerous to count as he does to Hagar in Genesis 16:10. Furthermore God will name or rename people like Abraham, Isaac, Jacob, Sarah, etc., but he will not be renamed by them. Along comes Hagar who maintains her humble maiden's name and she renames God. In Genesis chapter 16 we read: She gave this name to the Lord who spoke to her: "You are the God who sees me," for she said, "I have now seen the One who sees me."(Genesis 16:13 NIV). Wow! The God who sees the afflicted, the God who sees you and me, the God who sees purpose in the lowliest of the lowly. The lowliest of the lowly who sees God as the One, diverse, but unified.

God Is Speaking

There is not a plethora of God contacts to females in the book of Genesis. Most of those that come to mind are generally not of a positive nature perhaps because they come on the heels of some negative action. For example, when Eve is confronted by God in Genesis chapter 3 after she has eaten the forbidden fruit, it is an inquisition with a consequence of a rather harsh nature. Furthermore, it is the first sign of the introduction of epigenetics. Medically speaking this is one of those baffling scientific phenomena that is both a puzzlement to scientists and somewhat an embarrassment to them in that it does not fit their neat and traditional model of how traits are passed on to the next generation. But there you have it in that due to the transgression of Eve, all women from that moment henceforth will have pain in child bearing.

Perhaps we can recall the rather limited encounter that Sarah has with God. In Genesis chapter 18 we have the only time that God spoke to Sarah. It was a rather indirect encounter for the most part at that. Sarah is listening outside the tent when the Lord informed Abraham that he and Sarah would have a baby the next year, despite her advanced age. We are told that Sarah laughed to herself. Whether the actual laughter was heard by God or he discerned the laughter, we cannot say for certain. What is interesting is that God turns to Abraham and asks why Sarah laughed. Next after God points out that having Sarah conceive at an advanced age is well within his ability. Now she has what appears to be her first and only direct conversation with God. She shows fear. And she lies. She says she didn't laugh. God simply says "Yes, you did laugh". One conversation with God. She has 4 words and God has 4 words. Whatever our recollection of the encounter, there was no rebuke. Indeed, when everything comes to fruition and the baby is born, God himself decides that laughter would be a good name and thus Isaac is named. God actually speaks more to another female connected with Abraham, namely Hagar. The first encounter in Genesis chapter 16 predates the above encounter with Sarah. God finds Hagar when she is in the desert fleeing from Sarah who has mistreated her in a fit of apparent jealousy after Hagar conceived the baby that Sarah arranged. Abraham indirectly allowed this. God finds Hagar and in typical God fashion, especially with females, begins by asking a question. He tells her to return to Hagar and gives her a long blessing for her and her offspring. Later on Sarah will show irritation over the way that son of Hagar, Ishmael, treated her own son. She sends them both into the desert again. There is another God encounter where God, in the guise of the angel of the Lord, which, begins with a question. He then makes another pledge to Hagar and her offspring. So, in effect, we have 2 somewhat lengthy conversations and interactions between God and Hagar. These are explored in detail under the God Encounters chapter.

Women Of Ill Repute

In this section we will explore women of ill repute including by act of adultery, or promiscuity, or prostitution. We might also raise the question of how some seemed to have escaped this designation when they just as easily could have been given a negative connotation. We will also mention some whose story line may have included more than what is written in terms of innuendo and tradition that has been handed down with very little evidence and yet very much ingrained in the mind. Also, we might even call to question some of the actual existence of some of the women.

We have already written for this treatise an exposition on the book of Hosea and the prostitute Gomer. As you may recall Gomer was the prostitute that God told Hosea the prophet to marry. This was supposed to be a metaphor for the people of God as to how God perceived treatment towards himself just as the people of Israel had prostituted themselves before other gods. God then has Hosea impregnate her only to witness her return to her prostitution and become pregnant by others. Rich raises the legitimate question if Gomer was a real person or a very strong realistic symbol. After all, would God have one of his prophets marry such a woman, return to her prostitution ways, and then have Hosea buy her back?

The inverse of this comes from the woman who washed the feet of Jesus. This is one of the few stories that has some version in all four gospels. What is interesting is what is often associated with her is pure conjecture and speculation. In none of the gospels are we told that she was a prostitute or a promiscuous woman. In two of the gospels, she is critiqued not by Jesus, but by others because she used expensive perfume that could have been sold, and the proceeds given for charitable purposes. In the other two gospels, we are merely told that she was a sinner which the religious leaders suggested that Jesus should have known about and avoided her. The fact that the woman was someone with agency and resources may have contributed to her direct put down over time and indirect put down in which there is a conflation of all things bad attributed to women.

Another challenge with the conflation concept is when we look at the name Mary in the Bible. Mary in one of the stories of the women washing Jesus feet is very clearly the Mary from the Lazarus and Mary and Martha stories. She is not Mary Magdalene as sometimes people have supposed. Furthermore, Mary Magdalene has had many rumors about her over the years, including that she was a prostitute. There's absolutely not a shred of evidence that she was a prostitute. Yet the stories proliferate. What she does appear to be is the first person who saw Jesus at the grave, following his resurrection.

Another New Testament story is the story of the woman at the well. We recall that the disciples are hungry, and Jesus sends them into the city to purchase food. Meanwhile, a promiscuous woman approaches the well by Jesus and he requests some water from her. There is a healthy exchange, in which Jesus calls her out on her activities and yet does not condemn her even as he promises her living water. Perhaps the most famous adulteress occurs in John chapter 8, which story has been added to earlier versions of the text. In this story A woman caught in the act of adultery is brought to Jesus by the religious leaders in order for them to have permission to stone her to death like the law of Moses noted. Jesus refused to do so and yet does remind the woman to go and sin no more. See our more expanded version on this story in this treatise.

We have written in another section how Tamar in the Original Testament is one of only two women in the entire Bible with the designation of righteous. This occurs despite her deception to induce an in law into a sexual encounter by trickery and become pregnant. Check out the whole story and our version before you make judgments. Also, we have in the Original Testament Rahab who is a prostitute living in the foreign town of Jericho. The Israelites have come to claim the territory, but those Israelite spies are in jeopardy for their lives until Rahab hides them. There is a fair chance that she let out the Israelites spies through the same window that the local men went out secretly themselves. Arguably, they would not want to look there in order to make it avoid looking like they already knew such hidden exit strategy existed. The woman is arguably as wise as she is courageous.

Perhaps one of the most unusual twists in the Original Testament occurs with the story of queen Bathsheba. We are all familiar with the adultery relationship that she had with King David. Refer to our piece on this from our book on David, where we show that this was likely orchestrated among two elite individuals who knew each other well and the whereabouts of the other most of the time. Arguably, she was not only responsible for the death of her husband at least indirectly, but may well have contributed to the plot.

Bathsheba also may well have contributed to the defamation of her honorable general husband's reputation after his death as we wrote about in our book, David and Michelangelo. She was indeed a woman of agency. Furthermore, she is arguably the female figure in the book by Harold Bloom, entitled the Book of J. As such she would have had ample opportunity to influence history, and how it was told in subsequent generations. Conceivably it was her ability to influence the telling of history that led to the more positive versions of Tamar and Rahab. Please keep in mind that Tamar, Rahab, and Bathsheba constitute 3 of the 4 women mentioned in the linage of Jesus in the gospel of Matthew.

JESUS SOLICITS A WOMAN OF ILL REPUTE

Probably the last image that we would ever think of with Jesus is that he would solicit a woman of ill repute. That is exactly what happens in the fourth chapter of the gospel of John. The circumstances include that the disciples were not around and that Jesus himself was tired. Apparently, he was thirsty as well as he asked a Samaritan woman for a drink of water while the disciples went into town in order to buy food. This seems a little bit peculiar for the man who made it a reputation for making food multiply out of minimum supplies. Furthermore, elsewhere we understand that the disciples basically lived off of the goodwill of the people that they were preaching the gospel of love and forgiveness to. Apparently, they did not receive those benefits presumedly in their home country of Israel and now were in the land of Samaria.

Now that we perhaps have drawn you into the story let us see how Jesus was perhaps drawing this woman in even as he was asking her to draw up a glass of water. We are conditioned to believe that Jesus merely wished to make a point of inclusion for both foreigners and women. In order

for that to be accomplished there had to be a reference to a symbolic metaphor and a revelation. We must keep in mind that this woman who had known many men could not have known whether or not Jesus was soliciting her as it is possible that her answer in the ninth verse of chapter 4 was in part feeling out the situation.

Whatever her understanding of the question was or the intention behind the water, Jesus then references that if the woman knew who is asking for the water that she herself would have asked Jesus to give a living water. While the woman seems stuck on the literal interpretation because Jesus has nothing to draw of the water with, she does seem open to recognize the possibility that Jesus might have something greater to offer then the patriarch Jacob who was the one who established the well to begin with. Note the subtlety that the woman claims Jacob as our father and that Jesus does make any suggestion otherwise.

This beautiful volley back and forth between the literal and symbolic, between man and woman, between foreigner and native, between person of the world and person beyond this world continues. Jesus points out that anyone who drinks the water from Jacob's well will become thirsty again but not so with the water that he has to offer representing eternal life. The woman now asks Jesus for that symbolic water. Before Jesus will grant that request, he tells her to get her husband and come back. Jesus is indeed baiting the woman because he knows that the man, she is living with is not her husband and that additionally she has had five husbands before him.

Now the woman is exposed, and she proceeds to expose Jesus as a prophet. She then proceeds to do what any of us would do under the circumstances of being exposed for what we are which is to divert the conversation. She chooses the topic of religion and worship and cites the difference between the Jews and the Samaritans. Jesus then gives the recognized differences between the two approaches but points to a time coming when the true worshipers worship in spirit and truth which is what God seeks. He then notes that God himself is spirit and that the true worshipers must worship in spirit and truth.

The woman then recognizes that the Messiah will come and explain everything and in her own words everything to which itself implies inclusion. Jesus then arguably makes the first declaration himself that he is that Messiah. Later we learn that many of the other Samaritans from the town believed in Jesus because of the simple testimony of the woman that Jesus told her everything that she ever did. We might ask why this was so. Did others feel that they too would have their lives revealed and changed? Or did they come because they sensed that the woman was never judged for her past? Either way we sense that they wished to come to feel a part of the inclusion that involved in Jesus own words spirit and truth.

THE BIRTH OF FORGIVENESS NEW TESTAMENT

No one questions that forgiveness is an integral part of the gospel. Some argue that it is a force more powerful than love. Certainly, love cannot be complete or receive its full manifestation without the concept and practice of a deep forgiveness. On the one hand we can circumvent this section by noting that love, like forgiveness, ultimately comes from God. It would appear though, the thing is, God like expressions need to have some form of human representation in order for us to begin to understand and appreciate and perhaps ultimately express some of this ourselves.

The author of Matthew arguably sets the background for this human expression of forgiveness. In chapter 1 the author traces the genealogy of Jesus back to Abraham. What is most notable is that in addition to the patriarchs, David, and a number of lesser figures, we have the mention of exactly four women. It is five if we count Mary, the mother of Jesus. We maintain that it is no small note that Mary is introduced in a way that makes her more important than Joseph. In verse 16 of chapter 1 we read that Jacob was the father of Joseph, the husband of Mary of whom was born Jesus who is called Christ

Who are the other four women? Why are they listed? Is there any connection with Mary? The first woman mentioned in the genealogy is Tamar who was the mother of Perez and Zerah. To be clear these are children who were born of incest as we have detailed in our book on the patriarchs. The next is Rahab who was arguably the Madame of a brothel. The next is Ruth who was a foreign woman who arguably acquired her second husband by at least some form of solicitation if not more. Finally, we have the mention of the wife of Uriah. With that mention we note several considerations. First the name of Bathsheba was not mentioned. Was this because to mention the actual name was still too suggestive or an actual reminder of a scandal or was there another reason? Please refer to our book on David to explore this concept further. We maintain it is no small measure that Bathsheba is referred to in the genealogy as the wife of Uriah.

While some have written on the purposeful mention of the use these women to diminish the potential scandal that Mary was an unwed mother, that is not our purpose here. Nor do we maintain the extreme opposite position that a virgin birth through Mary was to elevate the position of all women regardless of their background. We do maintain though that these women may well be mentioned in order to show a connection that some would have pre-supposed existed with Mary.

In fact, Joseph himself believed that Mary had some type of illicit relationship before it was revealed to him that Jesus was conceived by the Holy Spirit. The evidence of this comes in verse 19 of chapter 1 of Matthew. We must keep in mind that while we the reader have already been told that the conception of Jesus was through the Holy Spirit, Joseph did not realize that in verse 19.

Rather we are told that he was a righteous man and did not wish to expose Mary to public disgrace and therefore was going to divorce her. This we maintain, was the first expression in the human flesh that Jesus was both exposed to and would have been aware of. In other words, Joseph had already forgiven Mary even though he did not need to. The implication of that may be quite offensive to our ears today to suggest that we need to practice such a radical forgiveness Even to people who have not necessarily sinned against us. While we may have short changed Joseph all these years without realizing that forgiveness, we should also consider that Joseph had to practice that forgiveness to others all of his life who still believed in the scandal of his wife. This may be lost on us but was certainly not lost on Jesus.

Washing Jesus Feet

If we are honest with ourselves, we sometimes find the paradoxes of the gospels and New Testament and the sayings of Jesus to be offensive. One of these offensive stories is found in all of the gospels making it once again somewhat of a minority, namely a story in which a woman washes the feet of Jesus with a very expensive oil.

The offensive conclusion is basically given in Jesus own words in which he effectively says that in order to love more that we must sin more or at least be bigger sinners. Let us look at the four Gospels to see what they have in common as well as their differences before we come around to the offensive challenge given above.

First all of the gospel's detail that it a woman who washed the feet of Jesus at a dinner. All of them have in common that someone objected to this use of the expensive oil when the money could have been used for a worthy cause such as feeding the poor. From here our memories may suffer from conflation in which we blend elements of the different Gospels together.

In Matthew, for example, the woman is unnamed, and the host is Simon the leper and the disciples are those who complain. In Mark, the most ancient gospel, it is once again an unnamed woman with no specific one named as a complainer but rather a vague reference to "some" while the host again is Simon the leper. In Luke the woman is specified as a sinful woman which is the only gospel to specify that type of background. The host, meanwhile, is a Pharisee named Simon, and he is ultimately the one who does the complaining.

Finally in John, the woman is Mary, presumedly the sister of Martha since both Martha and her brother Lazarus who were siblings of Mary were present. The host is unnamed, but we may presume that it may well have been Martha because she was the one who was serving. The complainer in that instance was Judas, the disciple who eventually betrayed Jesus.

This common story, as a note, may well give some insight into the angle that each gospel tends to emphasize throughout the rest of that gospel. Only Luke, however, includes the parable within the actual story. In that parable Jesus told a story about two people who owed a money lender some money. One owed a rather large sum which was

10 times as much as the other individual owed. The question Jesus raised to the host was who would love the money lender the most. The Pharisee host answered correctly, according to Jesus, that it would be the individual who owed the highest amount. In fact, he uses the phrase that he supposed it would be the one who had the bigger debt forgiven. Jesus next reply shows the wisdom of how he can turn things around with just the right word. Jesus is able to take our supposes as well as our judgments and turn them into something very positive.

The man may have had a hard time acknowledging the greater love because he had judged the woman prematurely and he issued a weak "I suppose" as his answer. Jesus plays off of that weak answer and proceeds to both acknowledge the woman's many sins, forgive them, and send her on her way in peace. In so doing he does not judge his host for his weaknesses. We would do well to go on the offensive and seek ways to expand our love not by committing additional sins but in forgiving those who have and send them in peace realizing we don't always know their motives.

Woman Caught In Adultery

The story of the woman caught in the act of adultery at the start of John chapter 8 may be offensive from several different angles. Indeed, the original formers of the New Testament were not certain as to whether to include this for perhaps many reasons. It may well be that they were offended by the various measures themselves. They may even have been offended that in this story Jesus allows the woman essentially to go free. Certainly, they would not have excluded the story because of its sexual nature. Indeed, the Jewish leaders in the story acknowledge reference to the Original Testament principal and law of putting the woman to death.

If we are honest with ourselves, we struggle with where to place the offense in the story. Our first inclination is naturally to be offended at the Jewish leaders who sought to display their brand of justice on this unfortunate woman. The very consideration of bringing her to be condemned before Jesus is despicable. It is indeed a misapplication of justice. We do not need to be any degree of feminist to be offended at the fact that the partner is not brought to the scene. Few people probably appreciate the fact that nowhere in the Bible whether the New Testament or Original Testament is an adulterous couple put to death. Perhaps the most famous example of such a couple being let off the hook is with David and Bathsheba.

There has been much speculation as to what Jesus wrote in the sand when the question about putting the woman to death. was placed to him. Never have we seen any consideration that said "bring me the partner" and then we can talk justice. For the record, we do not have any evidence that Jesus ever finished what he was writing in the sand, only that he began to write. Perhaps we are offended at those leaders because they interrupted him while he was writing and so we will never know those particular words of Jesus.

What we do sense, is that it is not natural to be offended at the woman whatever her actual actions and intent may have been. It does not even remotely dawn on most of us to be offended that Jesus actually never condemned the woman or even her actions. Furthermore, we may be troubled in that Jesus did not say that her action was actually a sin even, but only to go and sin no more. Even deeper in the recesses of our minds is the trouble that we sense when we recognize that Jesus did not officially forgive her. Why was this?

HAGAR AND FORGIVENESS

In the search for the first human to human forgiveness, many people make the case for Esau, who forgives Jacob after many years of being in exile from each other. Arguably this becomes the basis of example for Joseph, to forgive his brothers after they have sold him into slavery and subsequently, he suffers for many years before rising to the top and going to a position where he can literally save their lives. Perhaps a more primordial story worth looking at is that of Hagar.

We recall that Abraham has already been promised several times by God that he will be the father of great nations with many offspring too numerous to count before he has any children. Nonetheless, Abraham is a little bit anxious about the process and first believes that he is going to have to give away his inheritance to one of his servants. Next both he and his wife, Sarah have their doubts, and Sarah convinces him to have a relationship with her maid servant Hagar.

Abraham goes along with the arrangement and produces a son named Ishmael. The expressed purpose by Sarah was for Abraham to impregnate Hagar in order that Sarah could build a family through her. While Hagar was pregnant, there was some friction between her, and Sarah, possibly because of some taunting by Hagar and looking down upon Sarah. Sarah brings up charges against Hagar and reported them to Abraham. He then suggested that Sarah do with Hagar whatever she thought best.

The language is clear as to what happened next. Sarah mistreated Hagar, and accordingly Hagar fled. She goes to the desert where God tracks her down and tells her to go back to Sarah and that she will be blessed for doing so. God recognizes her misery and the challenges that her son ultimately named Ishmael will have with other people. Then she returns to Sarah with no pledge that there will not be any further abuse.

Before Hagar returns, Hagar returns to her owner Sarah, for potentially more challenges, Hagar has an interesting exchange with God. Keep in mind that God has renamed Abram into Abraham. He has also renamed Sarai to Sarah. However, we have in Genesis chapter 16 the only occasion in the Bible, where anyone renames God. She gives the name to God as the One who sees me. Perhaps this truncated version means the One who sees me and who has looked after me and who will continue to look after me.

Since the reference appears to be that there is only One who looks after her, we can naturally infer that it is not Abraham, who looks after her. It is not Sarah, who looks after her. Indeed, we believe that knowing the challenges that Hagar went through that we can make a case that she had to forgive not only Sarah at some level but also that she had to forgive Abraham. Perhaps we can make a case that God forgave her for her taunting, and that of her child later.

CONCLUSION

One afternoon, Rich and I were sitting around in our favorite Christian restaurant, enjoying a simple meal and fellowship. He had a copy of the outline for this book in his hands in the preliminary version. He brought up an interesting question about where would history have gone without these women and specifically what would the men in their lives have done without these women. For me, this becomes the chicken and the egg question as to the importance of the men for these women to at least achieve some recognition. Our section on parables sheds some reflections on the importance of men and women in telling the eternal story.

I encouraged Rich to write on this topic. It did get me thinking, though, about developing a hierarchy of the most important women in the Bible. Certainly, if we begin at the creation story and look at Sophia as the female wisdom present at creation, it would be hard to find a stronger influence. We have the reference of God at creation, making male and female in the "our" image implying that some female energy and spirit must be present in the original God head. We certainly cannot top that.

If we confine our search to women with physical and visible attributes, we open up a nice source of speculation. A person does not need to be Catholic to appreciate a very strong role for Mary, the mother of Jesus. We have mentioned previously, the several important women in the life of David who played pivotal roles in his legacy. Bathsheba likely had a very strong role in preserving and telling key portions of the story of David far above and beyond her seduction effort. Harold Bloom has detailed this nicely. The widow from Tekoa certainly plays a pivotal role for David. Arguably Abishag has some surprisingly defining moments for David.

We might pick some obvious strong feminine leaders such as Deborah who did not seem to have much need of the male factor to be very successful in her endeavor for the people of Israel. At the opposite end of the spectrum are a number of women of lowly status, who are exonerated by Jesus in the New Testament. We think of the woman at the well or the woman who washed Jesus' feet. Perhaps one of the most poignant stories is the woman caught in the act of adultery, who ultimately Jesus uses to turn the tables on those who would accuse.

There is no shortage of worthy women whether high status or low status could serve as our ultimate role model. We believe, however, that the case can be made for Hagar. Recall that she is the mistress or slave wife of Abraham and eventually has a child by Abraham in order to continue the lineage of Abraham. In fact, it is Abraham's wife Sarah, who arranges the relationship to produce the child that they did not have previously. Sarah and Abraham are unwilling to wait for God to do the God thing and give them the promised offspring.

Abraham proceeds to have offspring through the slave wife. Accordingly, Hagar represents the woman of color who has little choice in her relationship and who becomes abused on at least one level without any support system on this earth to back her. She becomes a forerunner for Jonah, who also tries to flee his circumstances and destiny. On the one hand, we can say that God will be heard and was indeed heard from in the case of Hagar. On the other hand, God is listening as well. God will hear the cries of Hagar and her child.

God will tell Hagar the words do not be afraid just as the angels give to mother Mary. In all of the Bible, there are many characters who are renamed by God. However, only Hagar renames God noting that God is the One who sees me. We also note that a case can be made for Hagar being the first human to practice human to human forgiveness. This forgiveness is subsequently present in the Jacob and Esau story as well as the story of Joseph and his brothers. Arguably, this is the same type of forgiveness that Joseph in the New Testament aims to apply for his own circumstances. Hagar also stands in for the lowly foreign women in the New Testament who sought healing from Jesus.

Hagar represents the lowliest of class of people. These are the type of people that Jesus came minister to. She represents every male and female who struggles with their desert experience where they may feel abandoned by God. This may have fostered courage in the women who saved the life of Moses. She may have inspired Moses himself to endure his desert experience. The same too, with the desert experience of Joseph. Like Hagar, Jesus chooses to go into the desert at the start of his ministry and face unknowns. Like Jesus, Hagar emerges from the desert with a vision and promise. Such is possible only when she can overcome her plight by forgiving her abusers and demonstrating the first rudimentary expression of human-to-human forgiveness.

www.ingramcontent.com/pod-product-compliance
Lightning Source LLC
LaVergne TN
LVHW041842070526
838199LV00045BA/1399